UNITED STAT
HISTORY ATLAS

NEW ENGLAND INSTITUTE
OF TECHNOLOGY
LEARNING RESOURCES CENTER

HAMMOND®
INCORPORATED
MAPLEWOOD, NEW JERSEY   07040-1396

31304310

Contents

LIBRARY OF CONGRESS CATALOG CARD NUMBER 93-79626
ISBN 0-8437-7470-3
PRINTED IN THE UNITED STATES OF AMERICA

Gazetteer of States, Territories and Possessions

State or Territory	Area (sq. mi.)†	Area (sq. km.)†	Population (1990)	Inhabitants per sq. mi. ††	Admitted to the Union	Settled at	Date
Alabama	52,423	135,775	4,040,587	79.6	Dec. 14, 1819	Mobile	1702
Alaska	656,424	1,700,139	550,043	1.0	Jan. 3, 1959	Sitka	1801
American Samoa	77	199	39,000	506.5	*Feb. 16, 1900	....	....
Arizona	114,006	295,276	3,665,228	32.3	Feb. 14, 1912	Tucson	1752
Arkansas	53,182	137,742	2,350,725	45.1	Jun. 15, 1836	Arkansas Post	1685
California	163,707	424,002	29,760,020	190.8	Sept. 9, 1850	San Diego	1769
Colorado	104,100	269,620	3,294,394	31.8	Aug. 1, 1876	Near Denver	1858
Connecticut	5,544	14,358	3,287,116	678.5	Jan. 9, 1788	Windsor	1635
Delaware	2,489	6,447	666,168	340.7	Dec. 7, 1787	Cape Henlopen	1627
District of Columbia	68	177	606,900	9,949.2	** 1790-1791	....	1790
Florida	65,758	170,313	12,937,926	239.6	Mar. 3, 1845	St. Augustine	1565
Georgia	59,441	153,953	6,478,216	111.8	Jan. 2, 1788	Savannah	1733
Guam	209	541	133,152	578.9	*Dec. 10, 1898	Agana	....
Hawaii	10,932	28,313	1,108,229	172.5	Aug. 21, 1959	....	....
Idaho	83,574	216,456	1,006,749	12.2	July 3, 1890	Coeur d'Alene	1842
Illinois	57,918	150,007	11,430,602	205.6	Dec. 3, 1818	Kaskaskia	1720
Indiana	36,420	94,328	5,544,159	154.6	Dec. 11, 1816	Vincennes	1730
Iowa	56,276	145,754	2,776,755	49.7	Dec. 28, 1846	Burlington	1788
Kansas	82,282	213,110	2,477,574	30.3	Jan. 29, 1861	....	1831
Kentucky	40,411	104,665	3,685,296	92.8	June 1, 1792	Harrodsburg	1774
Louisiana	51,843	134,275	4,219,973	96.9	Apr. 30, 1812	Iberville	1699
Maine	35,387	91,653	1,227,928	39.8	Mar. 15, 1820	Bristol	1624
Maryland	12,407	32,135	4,781,468	489.1	Apr. 28, 1788	St. Mary's	1634
Massachusetts	10,555	27,337	6,016,425	767.6	Feb. 6, 1788	Plymouth	1620
Michigan	96,810	250,738	9,295,297	163.6	Jan. 26, 1837	Near Detroit	1650
Minnesota	86,943	225,182	4,375,099	54.9	May 11, 1858	St. Peter's River	1805
Mississippi	48,434	125,443	2,573,216	54.8	Dec. 10, 1817	Natchez	1716
Missouri	69,709	180,546	5,117,073	74.3	Aug. 10, 1821	St. Louis	1764
Montana	147,046	380,850	799,065	5.5	Nov. 8, 1889	....	1809
Nebraska	82,282	213,110	1,578,385	20.5	Mar. 1, 1867	Bellevue	1847
Nevada	110,567	286,368	1,201,833	10.9	Oct. 31, 1864	Genoa	1850
New Hampshire	9,351	24,219	1,109,252	123.7	June 21, 1788	Dover and Portsmouth	1623
New Jersey	8,722	22,590	7,730,188	1,041.9	Dec. 18, 1787	Bergen	1617
New Mexico	121,598	314,939	1,515,069	12.5	Jan. 6, 1912	Santa Fe	1605
New York	54,475	141,089	17,990,456	381.0	July 26, 1788	Manhattan Island	1614
North Carolina	53,821	139,397	6,628,637	136.1	Nov. 21, 1789	Albemarle	1650
North Dakota	70,704	183,123	638,800	9.3	Nov. 2, 1889	Pembina	1780
Ohio	44,828	116,103	10,847,115	264.9	Mar. 1, 1803	Marietta	1788
Oklahoma	69,903	181,049	3,145,585	45.8	Nov. 16, 1907	....	1889
Oregon	98,386	254,819	2,842,321	29.6	Feb. 14, 1859	Astoria	1810
Pennsylvania	46,058	119,291	11,881,643	265.1	Dec. 12, 1787	Delaware River	1682
Puerto Rico	3,515	9,104	3,522,037	1,018.2	*Dec. 10, 1898	Caparra	1510
Rhode Island	1,545	4,002	1,003,464	960.2	May 29, 1790	Providence	1636
South Carolina	32,007	82,898	3,486,703	115.8	May 23, 1788	Port Royal	1670
South Dakota	77,358	200,358	696,004	9.2	Nov. 2, 1889	Sioux Falls	1856
Tennessee	42,146	109,158	4,877,185	118.3	June 1, 1796	Ft. Loudon	1757
Texas	268,601	695,676	16,986,510	64.9	Dec. 29, 1845	Matagorda Bay	1686
Utah	84,904	219,902	1,722,850	21.0	Jan. 4, 1896	Salt Lake City	1847
Vermont	9,615	24,903	562,758	60.8	Mar. 4, 1791	Ft. Dummer	1764
Virginia	42,769	110,771	6,187,358	156.2	June 26, 1788	Jamestown	1607
Virgin Islands	132	342	101,809	848.5	*Mar 31, 1917	St. Thomas I.	1657
Washington	71,303	184,674	4,866,692	73.1	Nov. 11, 1889	Astoria	1811
West Virginia	24,231	62,759	1,793,477	74.5	June 20, 1863	Wheeling	1774
Wisconsin	65,503	169,653	4,891,769	90.1	May 29, 1848	Green Bay	1670
Wyoming	97,818	253,349	453,588	4.7	July 10, 1890	Ft. Laramie	1834
United States	3,792,575	9,822,769	248,709,873	70.3	....	....	....

* Date of organization as Territory or acquisition by U.S.   ** Established under Acts of Congress   † Land and water.   † Calculations based on land area.

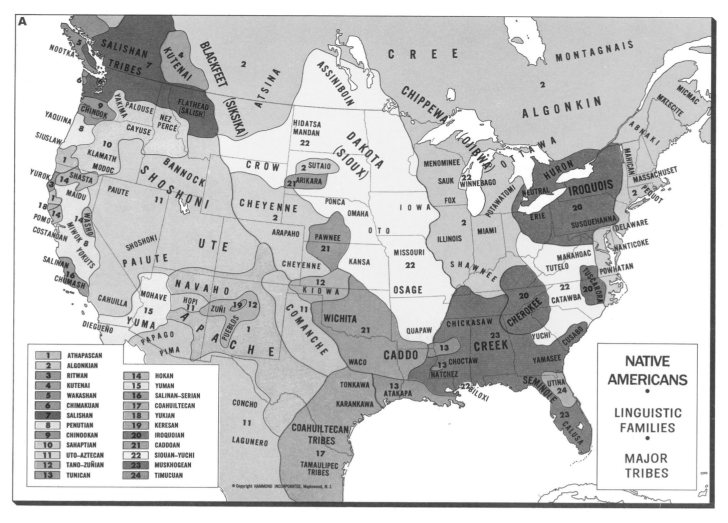

A

	ATHAPASCAN		
1	ATHAPASCAN	14	HOKAN
2	ALGONKIAN	15	YUMAN
3	RITWAN	16	SALINAN–SERIAN
4	KUTENAI	17	COAHUILTECAN
5	WAKASHAN	18	YUKIAN
6	CHIMAKUAN	19	KERESAN
7	SALISHAN	20	IROQUOIAN
8	PENUTIAN	21	CADDOAN
9	CHINOOKAN	22	SIOUAN–YUCHI
10	SAHAPTIAN	23	MUSKHOGEAN
11	UTO–AZTECAN	24	TIMUCUAN
12	TANO–ZUÑIAN		
13	TUNICAN		

© Copyright HAMMOND INCORPORATED, Maplewood, N.J.

NATIVE AMERICANS
•
LINGUISTIC FAMILIES
•
MAJOR TRIBES

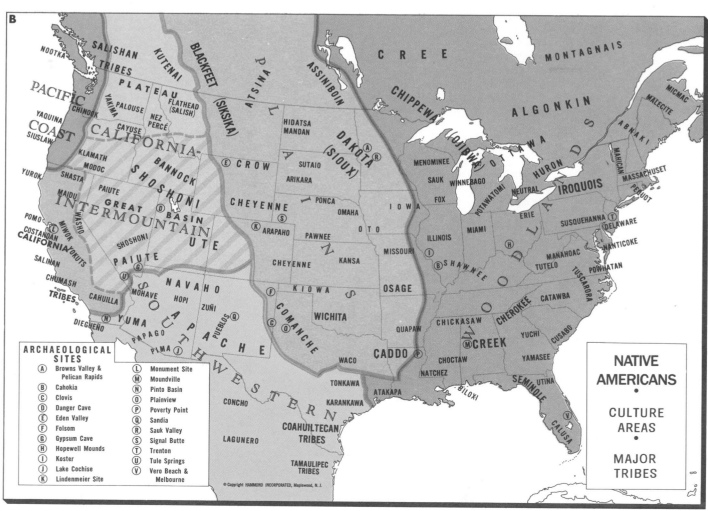

B

ARCHAEOLOGICAL SITES

(A)	Browns Valley & Pelican Rapids	(L)	Monument Site
(B)	Cahokia	(M)	Moundville
(C)	Clovis	(N)	Pinto Basin
(D)	Danger Cave	(O)	Plainview
(E)	Eden Valley	(P)	Poverty Point
(F)	Folsom	(Q)	Sandia
(G)	Gypsum Cave	(R)	Sauk Valley
(H)	Hopewell Mounds	(S)	Signal Butte
(I)	Koster	(T)	Trenton
(J)	Lake Cochise	(U)	Tule Springs
(K)	Lindenmeier Site	(V)	Vero Beach & Melbourne

© Copyright HAMMOND INCORPORATED, Maplebourne, N.J.

NATIVE AMERICANS
•
CULTURE AREAS
•
MAJOR TRIBES

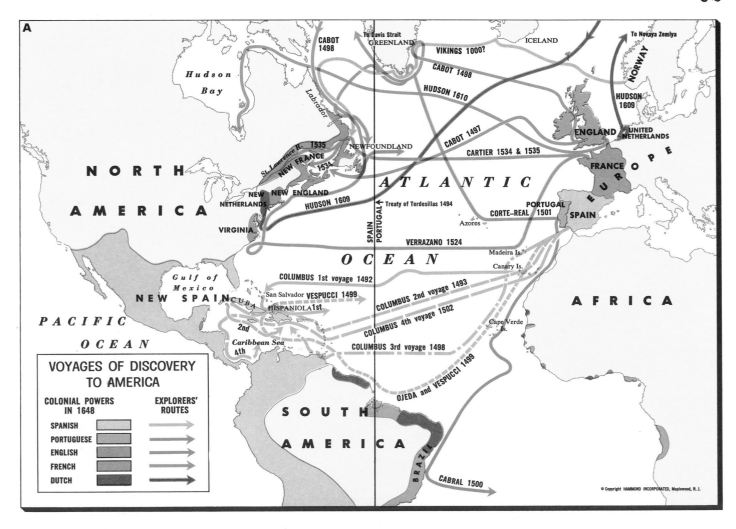

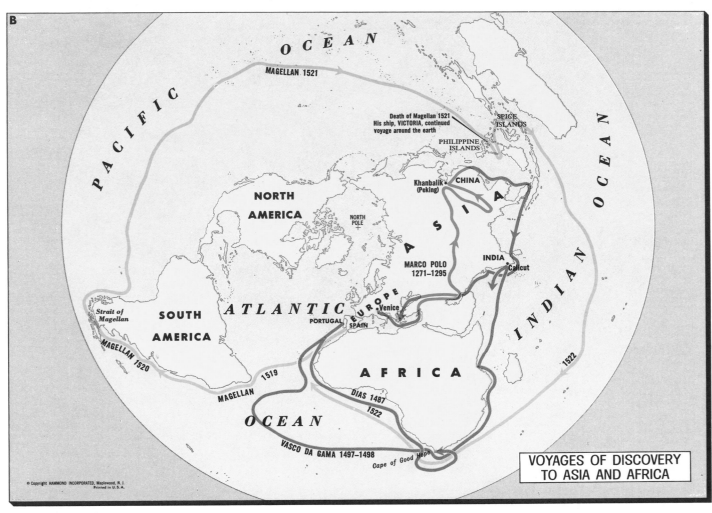

A

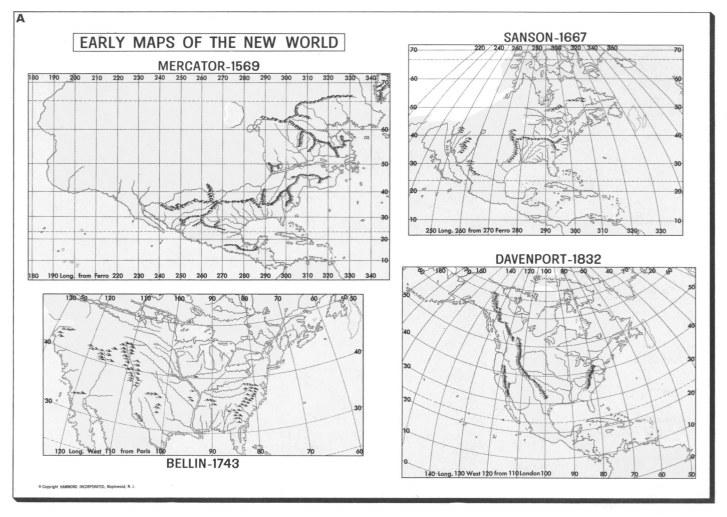

EARLY MAPS OF THE NEW WORLD

MERCATOR-1569

180 190 Long. from Ferro 220 230 240 250 260 270 280 290 300 310 320 330 340

SANSON-1667

250 Long. 260 from 270 Ferro 280 290 300 310 320 330

DAVENPORT-1832

140 Long. 130 West 120 from 110 London 100 90 80 70 60 50

BELLIN-1743

120 Long. West 110 from Paris 100 90 80 70 60

© Copyright HAMMOND INCORPORATED, Maplewood, N. J.

B

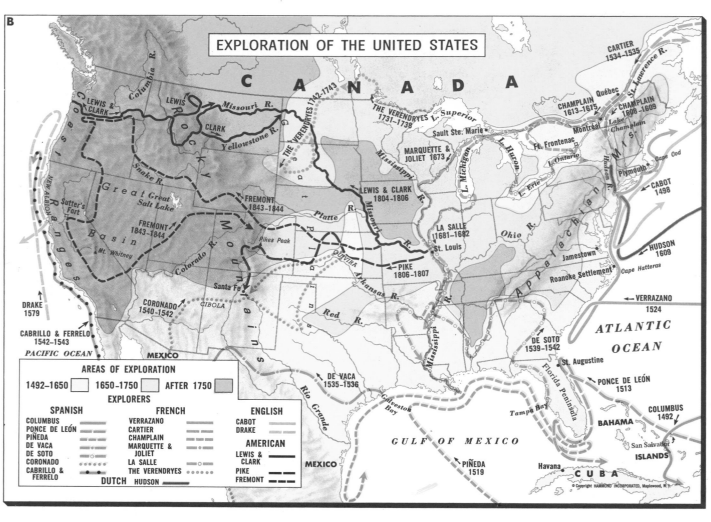

EXPLORATION OF THE UNITED STATES

AREAS OF EXPLORATION
1492–1650   1650–1750   AFTER 1750

EXPLORERS

SPANISH	FRENCH	ENGLISH
COLUMBUS	VERRAZANO	CABOT
PONCE DE LEÓN	CARTIER	DRAKE
PIÑEDA	CHAMPLAIN	
DE VACA	MARQUETTE & JOLIET	**AMERICAN**
DE SOTO		LEWIS & CLARK
CORONADO	LA SALLE	PIKE
CABRILLO & FERRELO	THE VERENDRYES	FREMONT

DUTCH HUDSON

© Copyright HAMMOND INCORPORATED, Maplewood, N. J.

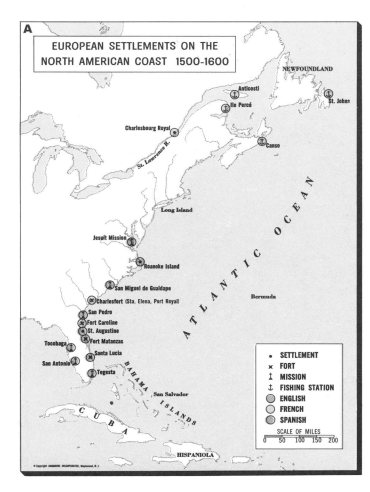

A

EUROPEAN SETTLEMENTS ON THE NORTH AMERICAN COAST 1500-1600

NEWFOUNDLAND

Anticosti
Ile Percé
St. Johns
Charlesbourg Royal
Canso
St. Lawrence R.

Long Island

Jesuit Mission
Roanoke Island
San Miguel de Gualdape
Charlesfort (Sta. Elena, Port Royal)
San Pedro
Fort Caroline
St. Augustine
Fort Matanzas
Tocobaga
Santa Lucia
San Antonio
Tegesta

ATLANTIC OCEAN

Bermuda

BAHAMA ISLANDS

San Salvador

CUBA

HISPANIOLA

- • SETTLEMENT
- ✕ FORT
- MISSION
- FISHING STATION
- ENGLISH
- FRENCH
- SPANISH

SCALE OF MILES
0 50 100 150 200

© Copyright HAMMOND INCORPORATED, Maplewood, N.J.

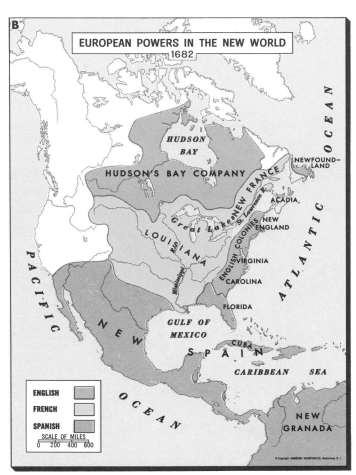

B

EUROPEAN POWERS IN THE NEW WORLD
1682

HUDSON BAY

HUDSON'S BAY COMPANY

NEW FRANCE

NEWFOUND-LAND

ACADIA

Great Lakes
St. Lawrence R.

NEW ENGLAND

LOUISIANA

ENGLISH COLONIES

VIRGINIA

CAROLINA

Mississippi

FLORIDA

GULF OF MEXICO

CUBA

NEW SPAIN

CARIBBEAN SEA

PACIFIC OCEAN

ATLANTIC OCEAN

NEW GRANADA

ENGLISH
FRENCH
SPANISH

SCALE OF MILES
0 200 400 600

© Copyright HAMMOND INCORPORATED, Maplewood, N.J.

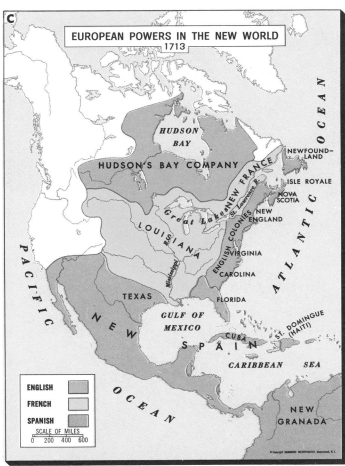

C

EUROPEAN POWERS IN THE NEW WORLD
1713

HUDSON BAY

HUDSON'S BAY COMPANY

NEW FRANCE

NEWFOUND-LAND

ISLE ROYALE

Great Lakes
St. Lawrence

NOVA SCOTIA

NEW ENGLAND

LOUISIANA

ENGLISH COLONIES

VIRGINIA

CAROLINA

Mississippi

TEXAS

FLORIDA

GULF OF MEXICO

CUBA

ST. DOMINGUE (HAITI)

NEW SPAIN

CARIBBEAN SEA

PACIFIC OCEAN

ATLANTIC OCEAN

NEW GRANADA

ENGLISH
FRENCH
SPANISH

SCALE OF MILES
0 200 400 600

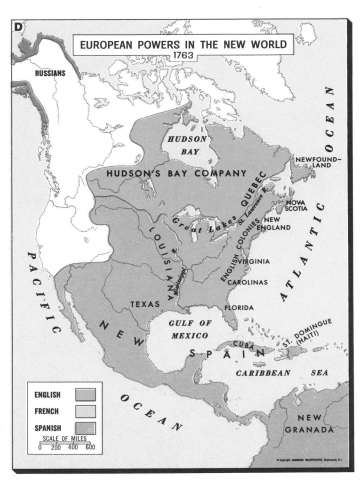

D

EUROPEAN POWERS IN THE NEW WORLD
1763

RUSSIANS

HUDSON BAY

HUDSON'S BAY COMPANY

QUEBEC

NEWFOUND-LAND

Great Lakes
St. Lawrence R.

NOVA SCOTIA

NEW ENGLAND

LOUISIANA

ENGLISH COLONIES

VIRGINIA

CAROLINAS

Mississippi

TEXAS

FLORIDA

GULF OF MEXICO

CUBA

ST. DOMINGUE (HAITI)

NEW SPAIN

CARIBBEAN SEA

PACIFIC OCEAN

ATLANTIC OCEAN

NEW GRANADA

ENGLISH
FRENCH
SPANISH

SCALE OF MILES
0 200 400 600

© Copyright HAMMOND INCORPORATED, Maplewood, N.J.

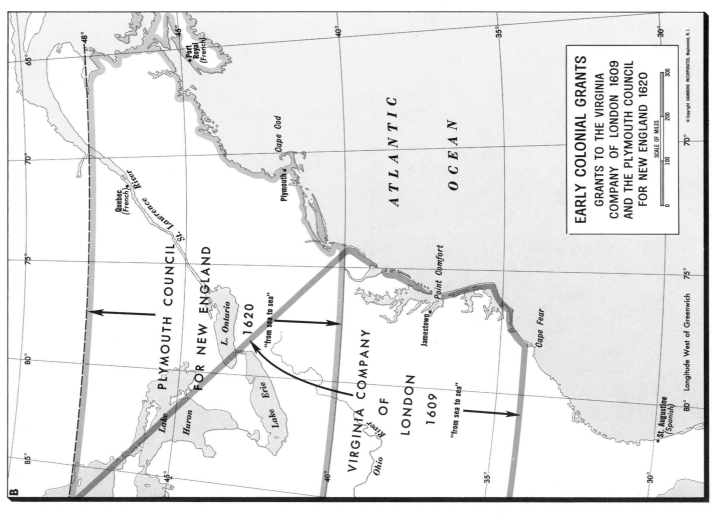

EARLY COLONIAL GRANTS
GRANTS TO THE VIRGINIA
COMPANY OF LONDON 1609
AND THE PLYMOUTH COUNCIL
FOR NEW ENGLAND 1620

SCALE OF MILES

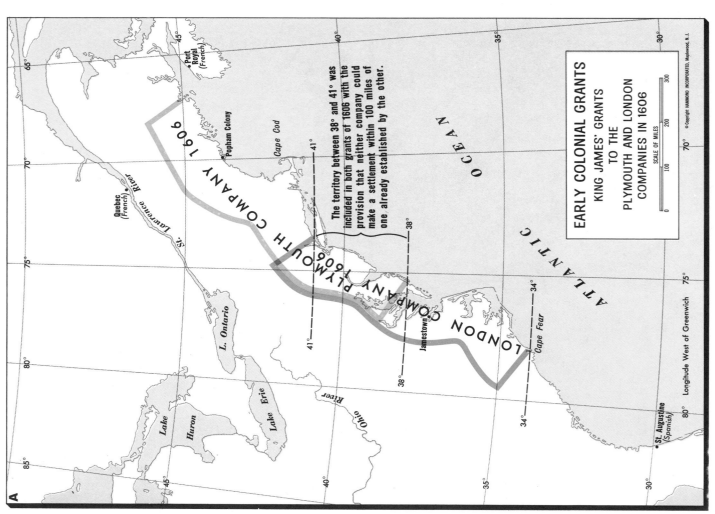

EARLY COLONIAL GRANTS
KING JAMES' GRANTS
TO THE
PLYMOUTH AND LONDON
COMPANIES IN 1606

SCALE OF MILES

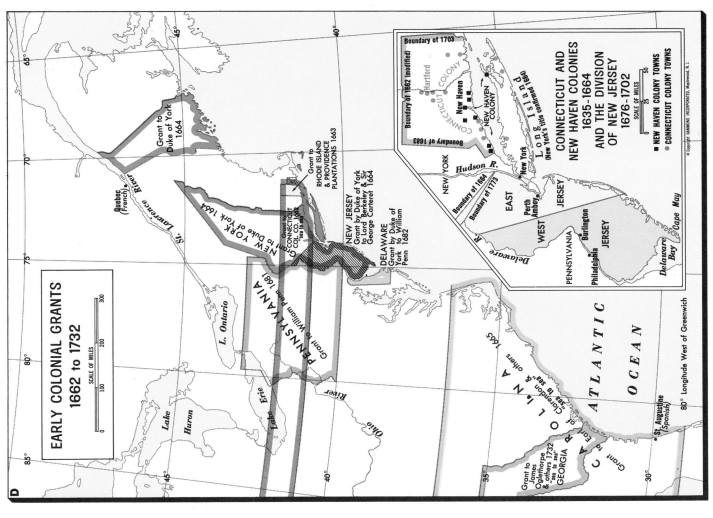

EARLY COLONIAL GRANTS 1662 to 1732

SCALE OF MILES

0 100 200 300

Quebec (French)

St. Lawrence River

L. Ontario

Lake Erie

Lake Huron

Ohio River

Grant to Duke of York 1664

Grant to Duke of York 1664

NEW YORK

CONNECTICUT COL. CO. 1662 "sea to sea"

Grant to RHODE ISLAND & PROVIDENCE PLANTATIONS 1663

NEW JERSEY Grant by Duke of York to Lord Berkeley & Sir George Carteret 1664

DELAWARE Grant by Duke of York to William Penn 1682

PENNSYLVANIA Grant to William Penn 1681

GEORGIA Grant to James Oglethorpe & others 1732 "sea to sea"

Grant to Earl of Clarendon & others "sea to sea" 1665

CAROLINA

ATLANTIC OCEAN

St. Augustine (Spanish)

80° Longitude West of Greenwich

CONNECTICUT AND NEW HAVEN COLONIES 1635-1664 AND THE DIVISION OF NEW JERSEY 1676-1702

SCALE OF MILES

0 25 50

■ NEW HAVEN COLONY TOWNS
● CONNECTICUT COLONY TOWNS

© Copyright HAMMOND INCORPORATED, Maplewood, N.J.

Boundary of 1703

Boundary of 1662 (modified)

Hartford

CONNECTICUT COLONY

New Haven

NEW HAVEN COLONY

Boundary of 1683

Long Island (New York's title confirmed 1664)

New York

Hudson R.

NEW YORK

Boundary of 1664

Boundary of 1773

Perth Amboy

EAST JERSEY

WEST JERSEY

PENNSYLVANIA

Philadelphia

Burlington

JERSEY

Delaware R.

Delaware Bay

Cape May

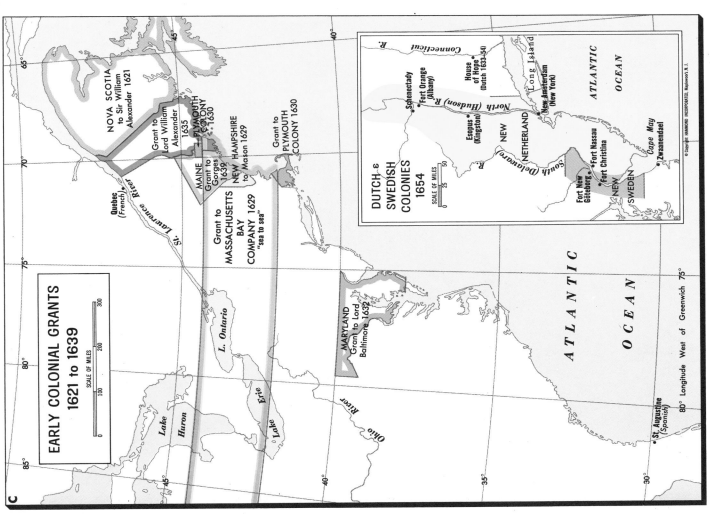

EARLY COLONIAL GRANTS 1621 to 1639

SCALE OF MILES

0 100 200 300

Quebec (French)

St. Lawrence River

L. Ontario

Lake Erie

Lake Huron

Ohio River

NOVA SCOTIA to Sir William Alexander 1621

Grant to Lord William Alexander 1635

PLYMOUTH COLONY 1630

MAINE Grant to Gorges 1639

NEW HAMPSHIRE to Mason 1629

Grant to PLYMOUTH COLONY 1630

Grant to MASSACHUSETTS BAY COMPANY 1629 "sea to sea"

MARYLAND Grant to Lord Baltimore 1632

ATLANTIC OCEAN

St. Augustine (Spanish)

80° Longitude West of Greenwich

DUTCH & SWEDISH COLONIES 1654

SCALE OF MILES

0 25 50

Connecticut R.

Schenectady

Fort Orange (Albany)

House of Hope (Dutch 1633-54)

Esopus (Kingston)

North (Hudson) R.

NEW NETHERLAND

Long Island

New Amsterdam (New York)

ATLANTIC OCEAN

South (Delaware) R.

Fort Nassau

Fort New Göteborg

Fort Christina

NEW SWEDEN

Cape May

Zwaanendael

© Copyright HAMMOND INCORPORATED, Maplewood, N.J.

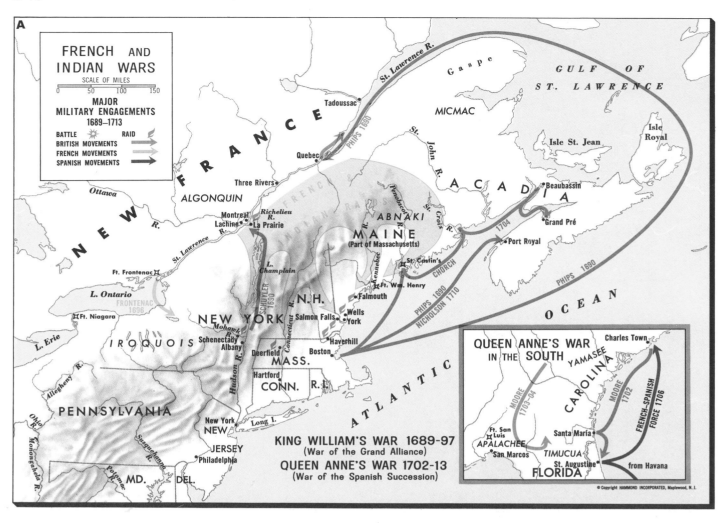

A

FRENCH AND INDIAN WARS
SCALE OF MILES
0 50 100 150
MAJOR
MILITARY ENGAGEMENTS
1689–1713
BATTLE ✶   RAID 🗡
BRITISH MOVEMENTS →
FRENCH MOVEMENTS →
SPANISH MOVEMENTS →

GULF OF ST. LAWRENCE

NEW FRANCE

Gaspe

MICMAC

Isle St. Jean

Isle Royal

ACADIA

Tadoussac

Quebec

PHIPS 1690

Three Rivers

ALGONQUIN

Ottawa R.

Montreal
Lachie Richelieu R.
La Prairie

St. Lawrence

Ft. Frontenac

L. Ontario

FRONTENAC 1696

Ft. Niagara

L. Erie

IROQUOIS

Allegheny R.

Ohio R.

Monongahela R.

PENNSYLVANIA

Susquehanna R.

Philadelphia

Potomac R.

MD.   DEL.

L. Champlain

SCHUYLER 1690

NEW YORK
Mohawk R.
Schenectady
Albany
Deerfield

Hudson R.

Hartford
CONN.

New York
NEW
JERSEY

Long I.

R. I.

St. John R.

St. Croix R.

Penobscot R.

Kennebec R.

ABNAKI

MAINE
(Part of Massachusetts)

St. Castin's
Ft. Wm. Henry
Falmouth

Salmon Falls Wells York

Haverhill

Boston

MASS.

N.H.

FRENCH INDIAN RAIDS

Beaubassin

Grand Pré

Port Royal

1704

CHURCH

PHIPS 1690 NICHOLSON 1710

PHIPS 1690

ATLANTIC OCEAN

KING WILLIAM'S WAR 1689-97
(War of the Grand Alliance)
QUEEN ANNE'S WAR 1702-13
(War of the Spanish Succession)

QUEEN ANNE'S WAR
IN THE SOUTH

YAMASEE

Charles Town

CAROLINA

MOORE 1703-04

MOORE 1702

FRENCH-SPANISH FORCE 1706

Ft. San Luis
APALACHEE
San Marcos

Santa María

TIMUCUA

St. Augustine

FLORIDA

from Havana

© Copyright HAMMOND INCORPORATED, Maplewood, N.J.

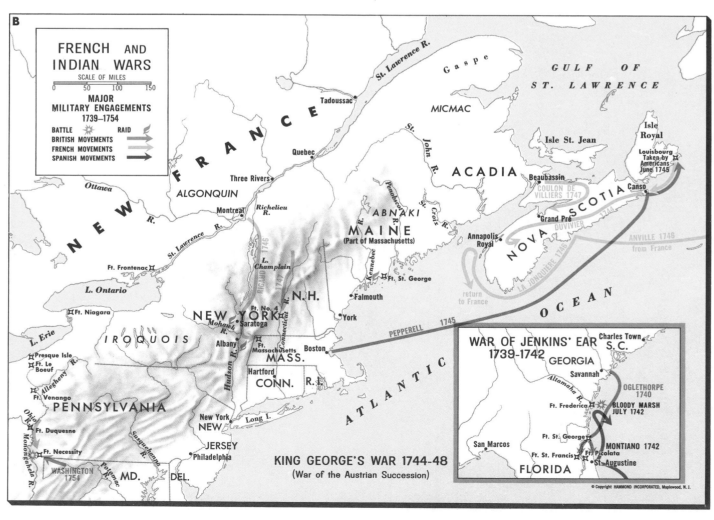

B

FRENCH AND INDIAN WARS
SCALE OF MILES
0 50 100 150
MAJOR
MILITARY ENGAGEMENTS
1739–1754
BATTLE ✶   RAID 🗡
BRITISH MOVEMENTS →
FRENCH MOVEMENTS →
SPANISH MOVEMENTS →

GULF OF ST. LAWRENCE

NEW FRANCE

Gaspe

MICMAC

Isle St. Jean

Isle Royal

Louisbourg
Taken by Americans
June 1745

Canso

ACADIA

COULON DE VILLIERS 1747

Tadoussac

Quebec

Three Rivers

ALGONQUIN

Ottawa R.

Montreal
Richelieu R.

St. Lawrence

Ft. Frontenac

L. Ontario

Ft. Niagara

L. Erie

IROQUOIS

Presque Isle
Ft. Le Boeuf

Allegheny R.

Ohio R.

Ft. Venango

Ft. Duquesne

Ft. Necessity

Monongahela R.

WASHINGTON 1754

PENNSYLVANIA

Susquehanna R.

Philadelphia

Potomac R.

MD.   DEL.

L. Champlain

RIGAUD 1746

RIGAUD 1747

NEW YORK
Mohawk R.
Ft. No. 4
Saratoga

Albany
Ft. Massachusetts

Hudson R.

Hartford
CONN.

New York
NEW
JERSEY

Long I.

R. I.

St. John R.

St. Croix R.

Penobscot R.

Kennebec R.

ABNAKI

MAINE
(Part of Massachusetts)

Ft. St. George

Falmouth

York

Boston

MASS.

N.H.

Beaubassin

Grand Pré

Annapolis Royal

NOVA SCOTIA

DUVIVIER 1744

LA JONQUIÈRE 1746

ANVILLE 1746
from France

return to France

PEPPERELL 1745

ATLANTIC OCEAN

KING GEORGE'S WAR 1744-48
(War of the Austrian Succession)

WAR OF JENKINS' EAR
1739-1742

Charles Town
S.C.

GEORGIA

Savannah

Altamaha R.

OGLETHORPE 1740

Ft. Frederica
BLOODY MARSH
JULY 1742

San Marcos

Ft. St. George

Ft. St. Francis

MONTIANO 1742

Ft. Picolata
St. Augustine

FLORIDA

© Copyright HAMMOND INCORPORATED, Maplewood, N.J.

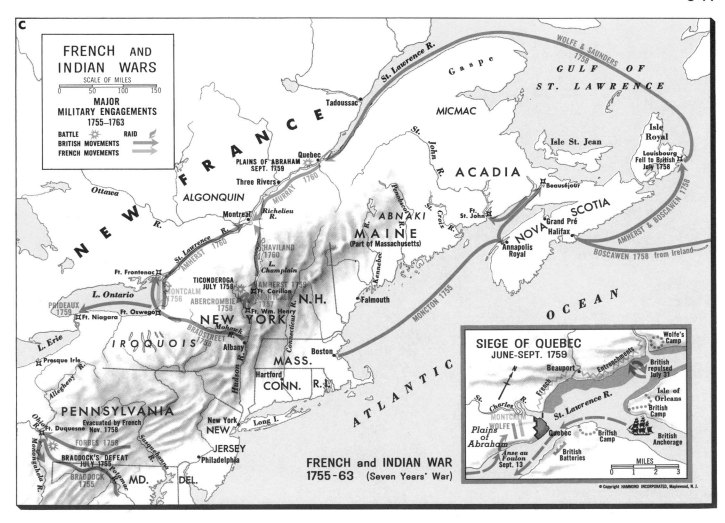

C

FRENCH AND INDIAN WARS

SCALE OF MILES
0   50   100   150

MAJOR MILITARY ENGAGEMENTS 1755–1763

BATTLE ✺   RAID ⚐
BRITISH MOVEMENTS ➡
FRENCH MOVEMENTS ➡

NEW FRANCE

St. Lawrence R.

Gaspe

GULF OF ST. LAWRENCE

WOLFE & SAUNDERS 1758

Tadoussac

MICMAC

Isle St. Jean

Isle Royal

Louisbourg
Fell to British
July 1758

PLAINS OF ABRAHAM SEPT. 1759
Quebec

St. John R.

ACADIA

Amherst & Boscawen 1758

Three Rivers

MURRAY 1760

ALGONQUIN

Montreal

Richelieu R.

St. Croix R.

Ft. St. John

Beauséjour

NOVA SCOTIA

BOSCAWEN 1758 from Ireland

Ottawa

St. Lawrence R. 1760

ABNAKI

Grand Pré
Halifax

Penobscot R.

MAINE
(Part of Massachusetts)

Annapolis Royal

Ft. Frontenac

AMHERST 1760

HAVILAND 1760

L. Champlain

Kennebec R.

TICONDEROGA JULY 1758
MONTCALM 1756
ABERCROMBIE 1758

AMHERST 1759
Ft. Carillon
MONTCALM

N.H.

Falmouth

MONCTON 1755

L. Ontario

Ft. Oswego

Ft. Wm. Henry

PRIDEAUX 1759

Ft. Niagara

NEW YORK

Mohawk R.

BRADSTREET 1758

OCEAN

L. Erie

IROQUOIS

Albany

Hudson R.

Connecticut R.

Boston

Presque Isle

Allegheny R.

MASS.

Hartford

CONN.

R. I.

ATLANTIC

PENNSYLVANIA

Ohio R.
Ft. Duquesne

Evacuated by French Nov. 1758

FORBES 1758

New York

Long I.

NEW

Monongahela R.

BRADDOCK'S DEFEAT JULY 1755

Susquehanna R.

Potomac R.

JERSEY

Philadelphia

BRADDOCK 1755

MD.

DEL.

SIEGE OF QUEBEC
JUNE–SEPT. 1759

Wolfe's Camp

St. Charles R.

Beauport

French Entrenchments

British repulsed July 31

MONTCALM
WOLFE

St. Lawrence R.

Isle of Orleans
British Camp

Plains of Abraham

Quebec

British Camp

British Anchorage

Anse au Foulon Sept. 13

British Batteries

British Camp

MILES
0   1   2   3

FRENCH and INDIAN WAR
1755-63 (Seven Years' War)

© Copyright HAMMOND INCORPORATED, Maplewood, N.J.

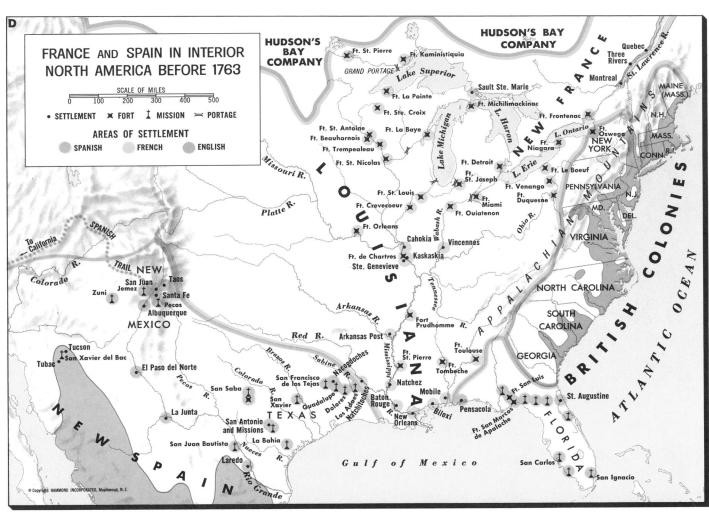

D

FRANCE AND SPAIN IN INTERIOR NORTH AMERICA BEFORE 1763

SCALE OF MILES
0   100   200   300   400   500

• SETTLEMENT   ✕ FORT   ⊥ MISSION   ⋈ PORTAGE

AREAS OF SETTLEMENT
⬤ SPANISH   ⬤ FRENCH   ⬤ ENGLISH

HUDSON'S BAY COMPANY

HUDSON'S BAY COMPANY

NEW FRANCE

Ft. St. Pierre

Ft. Kaministiquia

Quebec
St. Lawrence R.

GRAND PORTAGE

Lake Superior

Three Rivers

Montreal

MAINE (MASS.)

Sault Ste. Marie

Ft. La Pointe

Ft. Ste. Croix

Ft. Michilimackinac

Ft. Frontenac

N.H.

Missouri R.

LOUISIANA

Ft. St. Antoine

Ft. La Baye

L. Huron

L. Ontario

Ft. Oswego

MASS.

Ft. Beauharnois

Ft. Niagara

NEW YORK

CONN.
R.I.

Ft. Trempealeau

L. Michigan

Ft. Detroit

L. Erie

Ft. Le Boeuf

Ft. St. Nicolas

Ft. St. Joseph

Ft. Venango

PENNSYLVANIA

Ft. Duquesne

APPALACHIAN MOUNTAINS

MD.

N.J.

DEL.

Platte R.

Ft. St. Louis

Ft. Miami

Ft. Ouiatenon

Ohio R.

Ft. Crevecoeur

Wabash R.

SPANISH TRAIL

To California

Colorado R.

Ft. Orleans

Cahokia

Vincennes

VIRGINIA

BRITISH COLONIES

NEW

Taos

San Juan
Jemez

Santa Fe

Ft. de Chartres

Kaskaskia

Ste. Genevieve

Zuni

Pecos

Tennessee R.

NORTH CAROLINA

Albuquerque

MEXICO

Arkansas R.

Fort Prudhomme

SOUTH CAROLINA

Tucson

San Xavier del Bac

El Paso del Norte

Red R.

Arkansas Post

Ft. St. Pierre

Ft. Toulouse

GEORGIA

ATLANTIC OCEAN

Tubac

Pecos R.

Colorado R.

Braos R.

Sabine R.

Nacogdoches

Mississippi R.

Ft. Tombeche

San Saba

San Francisco de los Tejas

San Xavier

Guadalupe

Dolores

Los Adaes

Natchitoches

Natchez

Mobile

Pensacola

Ft. San Luis

St. Augustine

NEW SPAIN

La Junta

San Antonio and Missions

TEXAS

Baton Rouge

New Orleans

Biloxi

Ft. San Marcos de Apalache

FLORIDA

San Juan Bautista

La Bahia

Nueces R.

Laredo

Rio Grande

San Carlos

San Ignacio

Gulf of Mexico

© Copyright HAMMOND INCORPORATED, Maplewood, N.J.

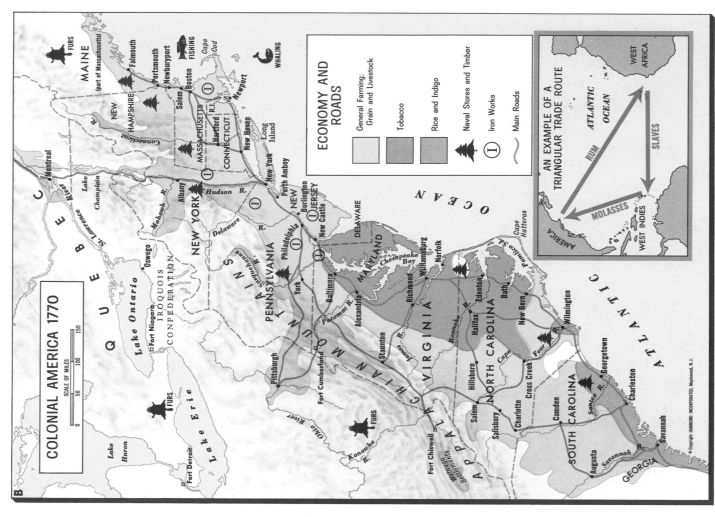

COLONIAL AMERICA 1770

SCALE OF MILES
0   50   100   150

ECONOMY AND ROADS

General Farming: Grain and Livestock
Tobacco
Rice and Indigo
Naval Stores and Timber
Iron Works
Main Roads

AN EXAMPLE OF A TRIANGULAR TRADE ROUTE

ATLANTIC OCEAN
WEST AFRICA
RUM
SLAVES
AMERICA
MOLASSES
WEST INDIES

FURS
FISHING
WHALING

MAINE (part of Massachusetts)
Falmouth
Portsmouth
Newburyport
Salem
Boston
Newport
Cape Cod
NEW HAMPSHIRE
MASSACHUSETTS
Hartford
CONNECTICUT
R.I.
New Haven
Long Island
New York
Perth Amboy
Burlington
NEW JERSEY
New Castle
DELAWARE
Philadelphia
Albany
Hudson R.
Mohawk R.
Delaware R.
Connecticut R.
Lake Champlain
St. Lawrence River
Montreal
QUEBEC
Lake Ontario
Lake Erie
Lake Huron
Oswego
Fort Niagara
IROQUOIS CONFEDERATION
NEW YORK
Fort Detroit
Ohio River
Kanawha R.
FURS
Fort Chiswell
Moravian Settlements
APPALACHIAN MOUNTAINS
PENNSYLVANIA
Pittsburgh
Fort Cumberland
York
Baltimore
Potomac R.
Alexandria
MARYLAND
Chesapeake Bay
Williamsburg
Norfolk
Richmond
James R.
Staunton
VIRGINIA
Roanoke R.
Halifax
Edenton
Bath
New Bern
Pamlico Sd.
Cape Hatteras
Wilmington
Cape Fear R.
Hillsboro
Cross Creek
NORTH CAROLINA
Salem
Salisbury
Charlotte
Camden
Georgetown
Santee R.
Charleston
SOUTH CAROLINA
Augusta
Savannah R.
Savannah
GEORGIA
ATLANTIC OCEAN

© Copyright HAMMOND INCORPORATED, Maplewood, N.J.

B

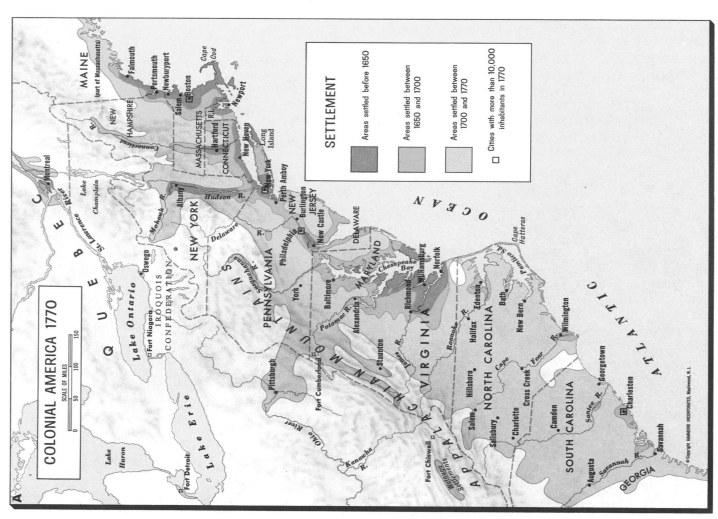

COLONIAL AMERICA 1770

SCALE OF MILES
0   50   100   150

SETTLEMENT

Areas settled before 1650
Areas settled between 1650 and 1700
Areas settled between 1700 and 1770
Cities with more than 10,000 inhabitants in 1770

MAINE (part of Massachusetts)
Falmouth
Portsmouth
Newburyport
Salem
Boston
Newport
Cape Cod
NEW HAMPSHIRE
MASSACHUSETTS
Hartford
CONNECTICUT
R.I.
New Haven
Long Island
New York
Perth Amboy
Burlington
NEW JERSEY
New Castle
DELAWARE
Philadelphia
Albany
Hudson R.
Mohawk R.
Delaware R.
Connecticut R.
Lake Champlain
St. Lawrence River
Montreal
QUEBEC
Lake Ontario
Lake Erie
Lake Huron
Oswego
Fort Niagara
IROQUOIS CONFEDERATION
NEW YORK
Fort Detroit
Ohio River
Kanawha R.
Fort Chiswell
Moravian Settlements
APPALACHIAN MOUNTAINS
PENNSYLVANIA
Pittsburgh
Fort Cumberland
York
Baltimore
Potomac R.
Alexandria
MARYLAND
Chesapeake Bay
Williamsburg
Norfolk
Richmond
James R.
Staunton
VIRGINIA
Roanoke R.
Halifax
Edenton
Bath
New Bern
Pamlico Sd.
Cape Hatteras
Wilmington
Cape Fear R.
Hillsboro
Cross Creek
NORTH CAROLINA
Salem
Salisbury
Charlotte
Camden
Georgetown
Santee R.
Charleston
SOUTH CAROLINA
Augusta
Savannah R.
Savannah
GEORGIA
ATLANTIC OCEAN

© Copyright HAMMOND INCORPORATED, Maplewood, N.J.

A

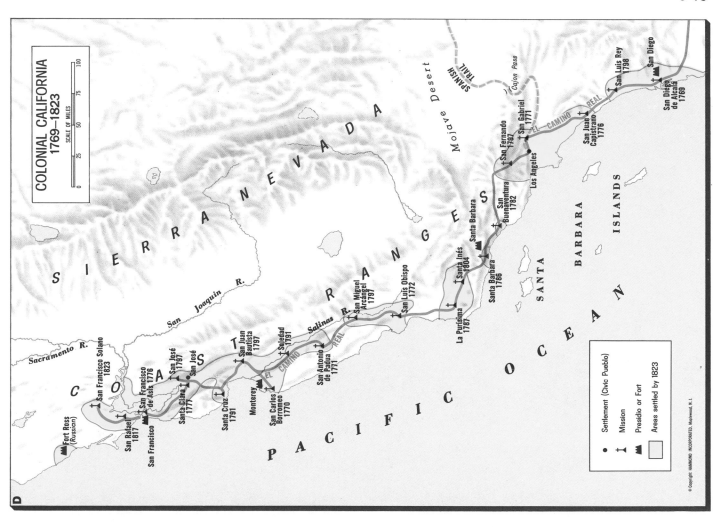

COLONIAL CALIFORNIA 1769–1823

SCALE OF MILES
0 25 50 75 100

SIERRA NEVADA

COAST RANGES

Mojave Desert

SPANISH TRAIL

Cajon Pass

EL CAMINO REAL

Sacramento R.

San Joaquin R.

Salinas R.

EL CAMINO REAL

Fort Ross (Russian)

San Rafael 1817
San Francisco Solano 1823
San Francisco de Asís 1776
San Francisco
Santa Clara 1777
San José 1797
San José
Santa Cruz 1791
San Juan Bautista 1797
Soledad 1791
Monterey
San Carlos Borromeo 1770
San Antonio de Padua 1771
San Miguel Arcángel 1797
San Luis Obispo 1772
La Purísima 1787
Santa Inés 1804
Santa Barbara 1786
San Buenaventura 1782
Santa Barbara
San Fernando 1797
San Gabriel 1771
Los Angeles
San Juan Capistrano 1776
San Luis Rey 1798
San Diego
San Diego de Alcalá 1769

PACIFIC OCEAN

SANTA BARBARA ISLANDS

Legend:
- Settlement (Civic Pueblo) •
- Mission ✝
- Presidio or Fort ▲
- Areas settled by 1823 ▢

© Copyright HAMMOND INCORPORATED, Maplewood, N.J.

D

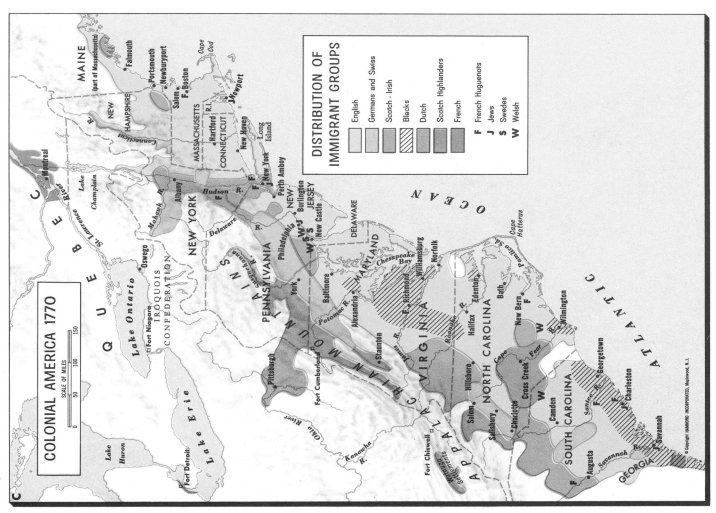

COLONIAL AMERICA 1770

SCALE OF MILES
0 50 100 150

DISTRIBUTION OF IMMIGRANT GROUPS

- English
- Germans and Swiss
- Scotch-Irish
- Blacks
- Dutch
- Scotch Highlanders
- French
- **F** French Huguenots
- **J** Jews
- **S** Swedes
- **W** Welsh

QUEBEC

Lake Huron
Lake Erie
Lake Ontario
Lake Champlain

Montreal
St. Lawrence River

Fort Detroit
Fort Niagara
Oswego

IROQUOIS CONFEDERATION

Pittsburgh
Ohio River
Kanawha R.
Fort Cumberland
Fort Chiswell

MAINE (part of Massachusetts)
Falmouth
Portsmouth
NEW HAMPSHIRE
Newburyport
Salem
F Boston
Cape Cod
MASSACHUSETTS
Hartford
New Haven
CONNECTICUT
R.I.
F Newport
Long Island

Connecticut R.
Hudson R.
Mohawk R.
Albany
NEW YORK
New York
Perth Amboy
NEW JERSEY
Burlington
New Castle
Delaware R.
Philadelphia
W,S,J
York
PENNSYLVANIA
Susquehanna R.

APPALACHIAN MOUNTAINS

Baltimore
MARYLAND
Potomac R.
Alexandria
DELAWARE
Chesapeake Bay
Williamsburg
F Richmond
Norfolk
Staunton
VIRGINIA
James R.
Roanoke R.
Halifax
Edenton
Bath
Cape Hatteras
Pamlico Sd.

Salem
Salisbury
Charlotte
Hillsboro
Crass Creek
NORTH CAROLINA
New Bern
Cape Fear R.
W
Wilmington

Augusta
Camden
Saluda R.
Senaca R.
SOUTH CAROLINA
F Georgetown
F Charleston
Savannah R.
GEORGIA
F Savannah

ATLANTIC OCEAN

© Copyright HAMMOND INCORPORATED, Maplewood, N.J.

C

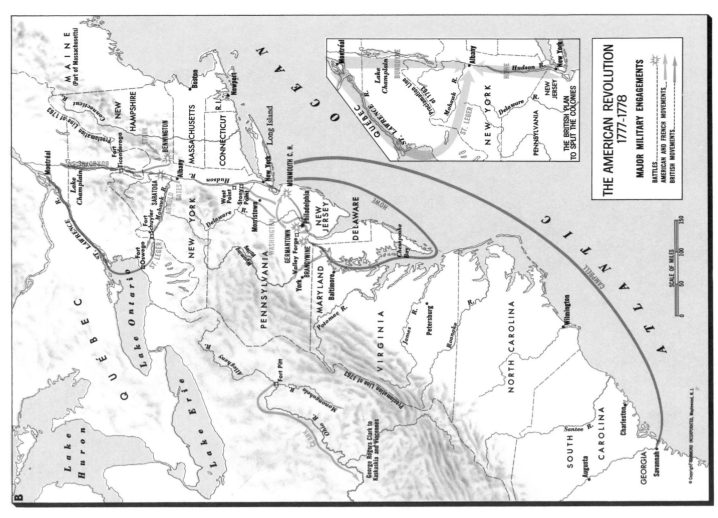

THE AMERICAN REVOLUTION
1777-1778

MAJOR MILITARY ENGAGEMENTS

BATTLES
AMERICAN AND FRENCH MOVEMENTS
BRITISH MOVEMENTS

THE BRITISH PLAN
TO SPLIT THE COLONIES

SCALE OF MILES
0   50   100   150

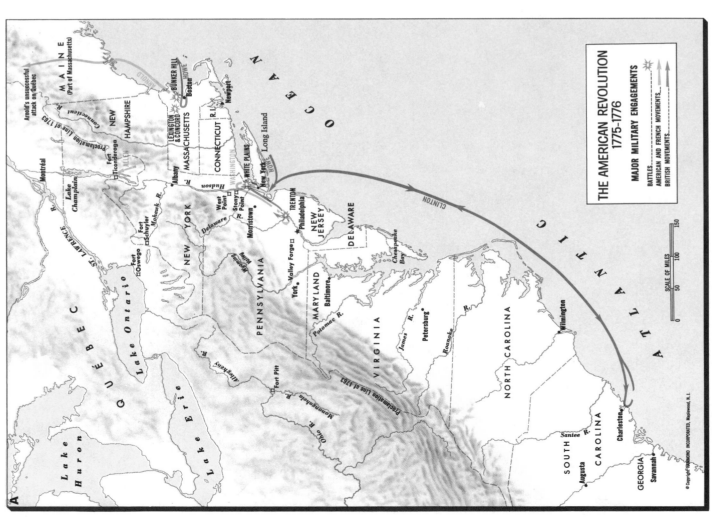

THE AMERICAN REVOLUTION
1775-1776

MAJOR MILITARY ENGAGEMENTS

BATTLES
AMERICAN AND FRENCH MOVEMENTS
BRITISH MOVEMENTS

SCALE OF MILES
0   50   100   150

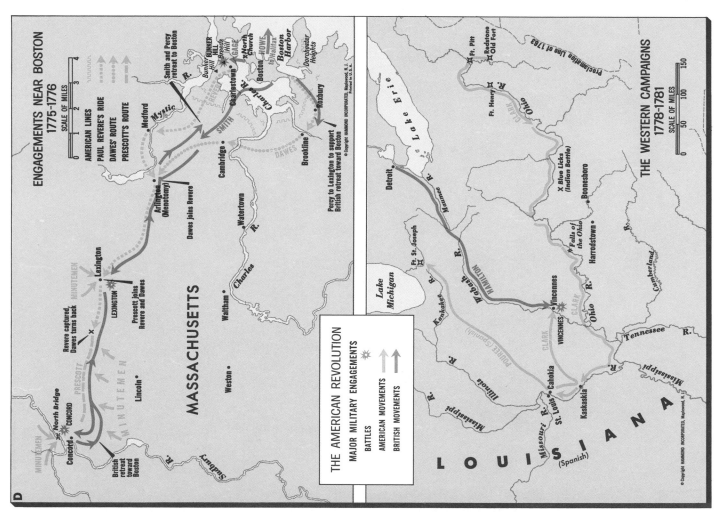

ENGAGEMENTS NEAR BOSTON
1775-1776

SCALE OF MILES
0 1 2 3 4

AMERICAN LINES
PAUL REVERE'S RIDE
DAWES' ROUTE
PRESCOTT'S ROUTE

MASSACHUSETTS

North Bridge
Concord
Lincoln
Lexington
Arlington (Menotomy)
Medford
Mystic R.
Cambridge
Watertown
Charles R.
Waltham
Weston
Sudbury R.

MINUTEMEN

Revere captured, Dawes turns back
Prescott joins Revere and Dawes
Dawes joins Revere
British retreat toward Boston

SMITH
HOWE
GAGE
Bunker Hill
Breed's Hill
North Church
Charlestown
Boston
Boston Harbor
Dorchester Heights
Roxbury
Brookline

Smith and Percy retreat to Boston
Percy to Lexington to support British retreat toward Boston

THE AMERICAN REVOLUTION
MAJOR MILITARY ENGAGEMENTS
BATTLES
AMERICAN MOVEMENTS
BRITISH MOVEMENTS

THE WESTERN CAMPAIGNS
1778-1781
SCALE OF MILES
0 50 100 150

Lake Erie
Lake Michigan
Detroit
Ft. Pitt
Redstone Old Fort
Ft. Henry
Ohio R.
Proclamation Line of 1763
Maumee R.
X Blue Licks (Indian Battle)
Boonesboro
Harrodstown
Falls of the Ohio
Ft. St. Joseph
Wabash R.
Kaskaskia R.
Kankakee R.
Illinois R.
HAMILTON
CLARK
Vincennes
VINCENNES
Cahokia
St. Louis
Kaskaskia
POUPEE (Spanish)
Missouri R.
Mississippi R.
Tennessee R.
Cumberland R.
Ohio R.

LOUISIANA (Spanish)

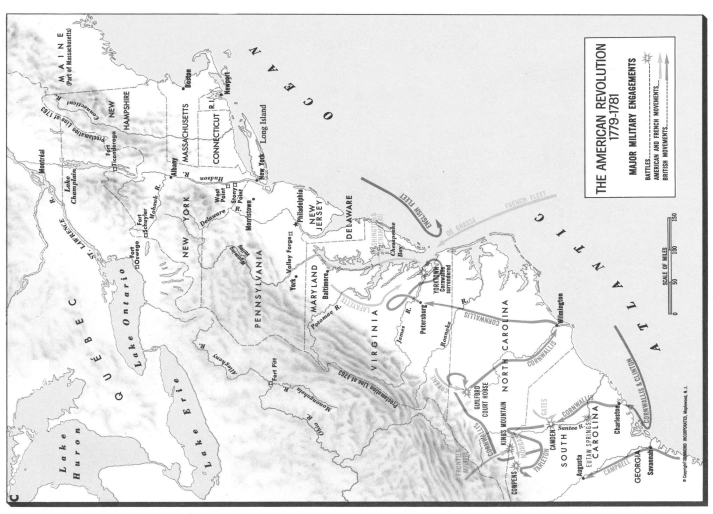

THE AMERICAN REVOLUTION
1779-1781
MAJOR MILITARY ENGAGEMENTS
BATTLES
AMERICAN AND FRENCH MOVEMENTS
BRITISH MOVEMENTS
SCALE OF MILES
0 50 100 150

Lake Huron
Lake Ontario
Lake Erie
QUÉBEC
MAINE (Part of Massachusetts)
NEW HAMPSHIRE
NEW YORK
MASSACHUSETTS
Boston
CONNECTICUT
R.I. Newport
Long Island
New York
Montréal
Lake Champlain
Fort Ticonderoga
Albany
Hudson R.
Mohawk R.
Fort Schuyler
Fort Oswego
West Point
Stony Point
Morristown
Philadelphia
NEW JERSEY
DELAWARE
Valley Forge
PENNSYLVANIA
Fort Pitt
Allegheny R.
Monongahela R.
Ohio R.
York
MARYLAND
Baltimore
Potomac R.
VIRGINIA
Petersburg
James R.
Roanoke R.
NORTH CAROLINA
Wilmington
GUILFORD COURT HOUSE
KINGS MOUNTAIN
SOUTH CAROLINA
Camden
Santee R.
EUTAW SPRINGS
COWPENS
TARLETON
Charleston
Augusta
GEORGIA
Savannah
CORNWALLIS
GREENE
GATES
CAMPBELL
YORKTOWN Cornwallis surrendered
LAFAYETTE
Chesapeake Bay
DE GRASSE
ENGLISH FLEET
FRENCH FLEET
ATLANTIC OCEAN
Proclamation Line of 1763
CORNWALLIS & CLINTON

A

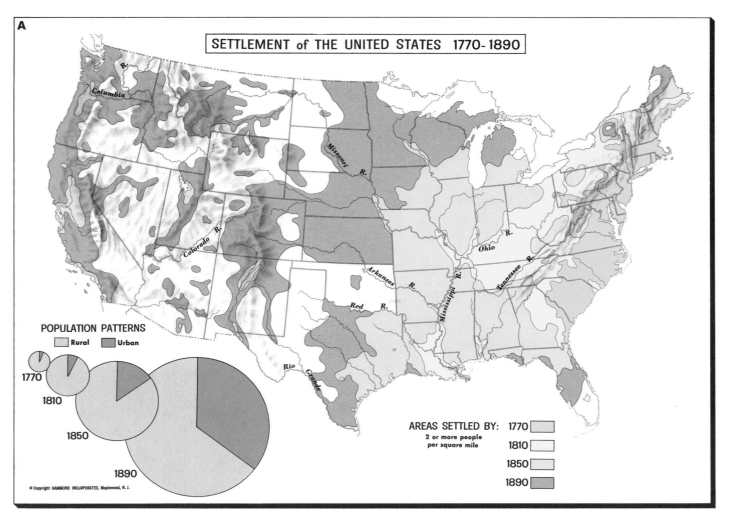

SETTLEMENT of THE UNITED STATES 1770-1890

POPULATION PATTERNS

Rural   Urban

1770
1810
1850
1890

© Copyright HAMMOND INCORPORATED, Maplewood, N.J.

AREAS SETTLED BY:
2 or more people per square mile

1770
1810
1850
1890

B

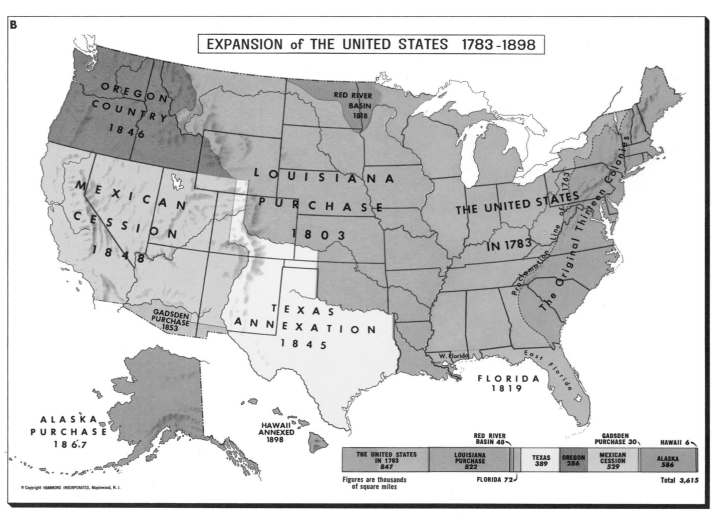

EXPANSION of THE UNITED STATES 1783-1898

OREGON COUNTRY 1846

RED RIVER BASIN 1818

LOUISIANA PURCHASE 1803

THE UNITED STATES IN 1783

The Original Thirteen Colonies

MEXICAN CESSION 1848

Proclamation Line of 1763

GADSDEN PURCHASE 1853

TEXAS ANNEXATION 1845

W. Florida

East Florida

FLORIDA 1819

ALASKA PURCHASE 1867

HAWAII ANNEXED 1898

© Copyright HAMMOND INCORPORATED, Maplewood, N.J.

THE UNITED STATES IN 1783 847	LOUISIANA PURCHASE 822	TEXAS 389	OREGON 286	MEXICAN CESSION 529	ALASKA 586

RED RIVER BASIN 48

GADSDEN PURCHASE 30

HAWAII 6

Figures are thousands of square miles

FLORIDA 72

Total 3,615

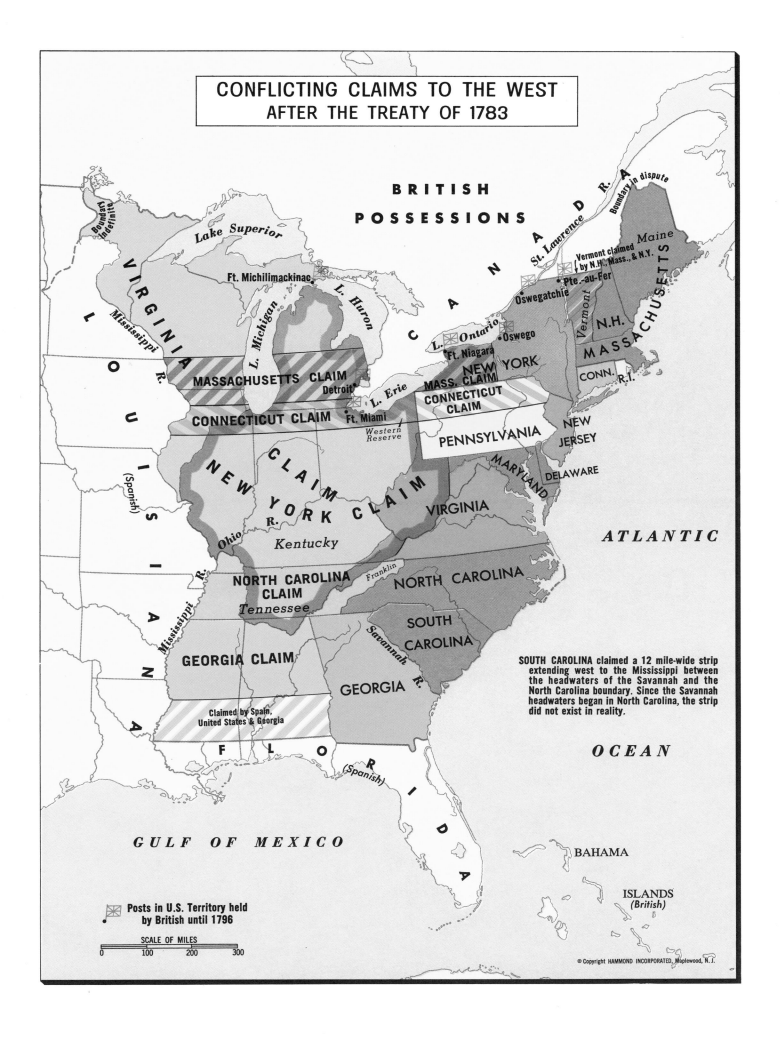

CONFLICTING CLAIMS TO THE WEST
AFTER THE TREATY OF 1783

BRITISH POSSESSIONS

C A N A D A

Boundary in dispute

Lake Superior

Ft. Michilimackinac

L. Huron

St. Lawrence

Maine

Vermont claimed by N.H., Mass., & N.Y.

Pte.-au-Fer

Oswegatchie

Vermont

N.H.

MASSACHUSETTS

VIRGINIA

Mississippi R.

L. Michigan

L. Ontario

Oswego

Ft. Niagara

NEW YORK

CONN.

R.I.

MASSACHUSETTS CLAIM

Detroit

L. Erie

MASS. CLAIM

CONNECTICUT CLAIM

Ft. Miami

Western Reserve

CONNECTICUT CLAIM

PENNSYLVANIA

NEW JERSEY

MARYLAND

DELAWARE

L O U I S I A N A

(Spanish)

NEW YORK CLAIM

Ohio R.

Kentucky

VIRGINIA

ATLANTIC

NORTH CAROLINA CLAIM

Franklin

NORTH CAROLINA

Tennessee

Mississippi R.

SOUTH CAROLINA

GEORGIA CLAIM

Savannah R.

GEORGIA

SOUTH CAROLINA claimed a 12 mile-wide strip extending west to the Mississippi between the headwaters of the Savannah and the North Carolina boundary. Since the Savannah headwaters began in North Carolina, the strip did not exist in reality.

OCEAN

Claimed by Spain, United States & Georgia

F L O R I D A

(Spanish)

GULF OF MEXICO

BAHAMA

ISLANDS (British)

Boundary Indefinite

Posts in U.S. Territory held by British until 1796

SCALE OF MILES

0   100   200   300

© Copyright HAMMOND INCORPORATED, Maplewood, N.J.

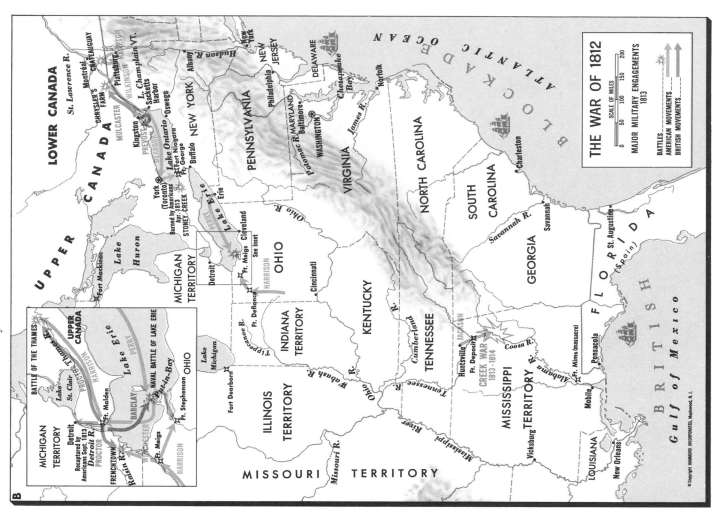

THE WAR OF 1812

SCALE OF MILES

0 50 100 150 200

MAJOR MILITARY ENGAGEMENTS
1813

BATTLES
AMERICAN MOVEMENTS
BRITISH MOVEMENTS

Copyright HAMMOND INCORPORATED, Maplewood, N.J.

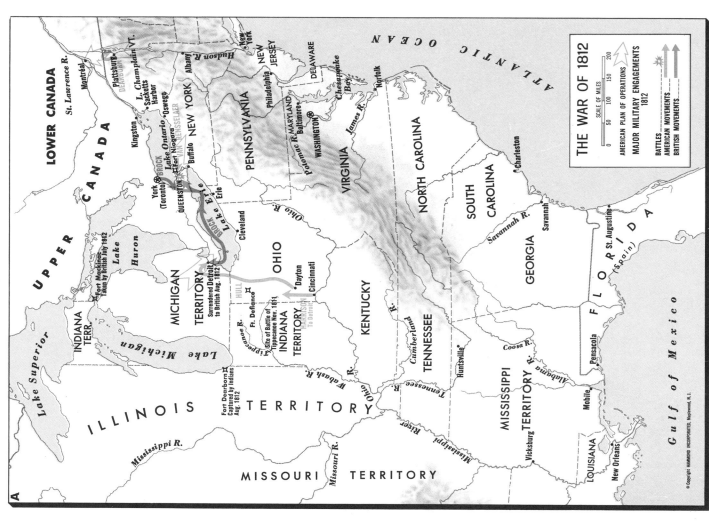

THE WAR OF 1812

SCALE OF MILES

0 50 100 150 200

AMERICAN PLAN OF OPERATIONS

MAJOR MILITARY ENGAGEMENTS
1812

BATTLES
AMERICAN MOVEMENTS
BRITISH MOVEMENTS

Copyright HAMMOND INCORPORATED, Maplewood, N.J.

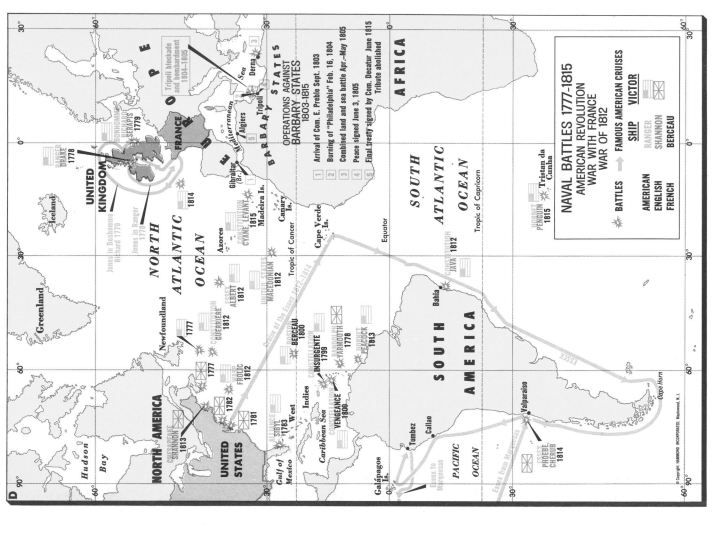

NAVAL BATTLES 1777-1815
AMERICAN REVOLUTION
WAR WITH FRANCE
WAR OF 1812

BATTLES	FAMOUS AMERICAN CRUISES
✳	→

	SHIP	VICTOR
AMERICAN	RANGER	
ENGLISH	SHANNON	
FRENCH	BERCEAU	

OPERATIONS AGAINST BARBARY STATES
1803-1815

1 Arrival of Com. E. Preble Sept. 1803
2 Burning of "Philadelphia" Feb. 16, 1804
3 Combined land and sea battle Apr.–May 1805
4 Peace signed June 3, 1805
5 Final treaty signed by Com. Decatur June 1815
     Tribute abolished

Tripoli blockade and bombardment 1804-1805

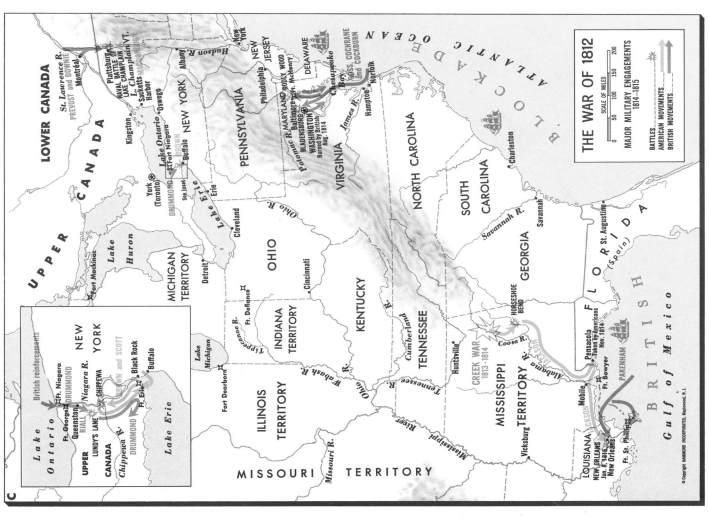

THE WAR OF 1812

SCALE OF MILES
0 50 100 150 200

MAJOR MILITARY ENGAGEMENTS
1814-1815

BATTLES	✳
AMERICAN MOVEMENTS	
BRITISH MOVEMENTS	

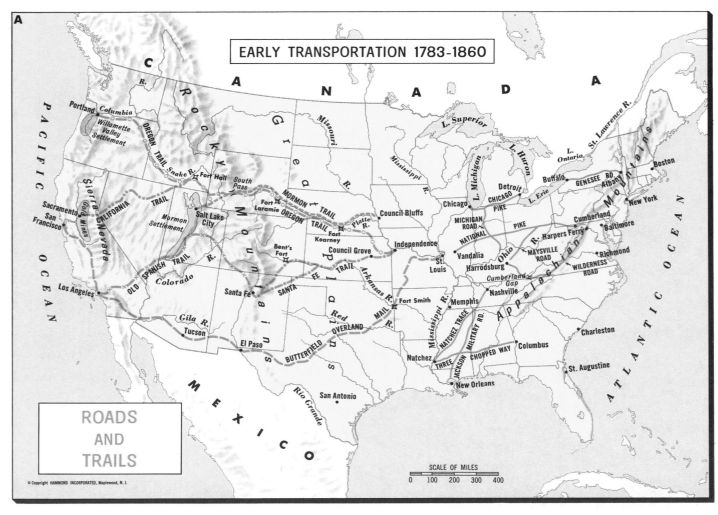

A

EARLY TRANSPORTATION 1783-1860

ROADS
AND
TRAILS

© Copyright HAMMOND INCORPORATED, Maplewood, N.J.

SCALE OF MILES
0   100   200   300   400

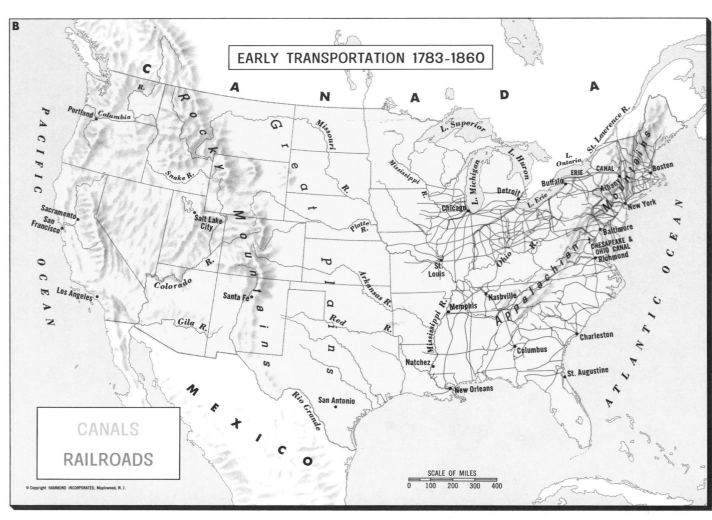

B

EARLY TRANSPORTATION 1783-1860

CANALS
RAILROADS

© Copyright HAMMOND INCORPORATED, Maplewood, N.J.

SCALE OF MILES
0   100   200   300   400

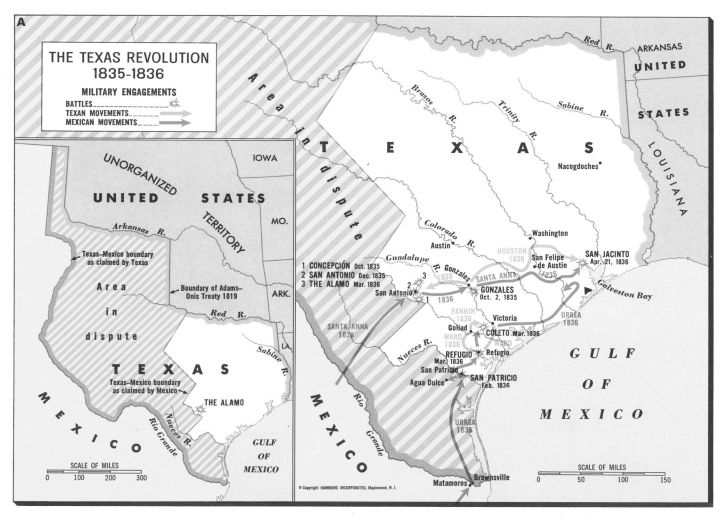

A — THE TEXAS REVOLUTION 1835-1836

MILITARY ENGAGEMENTS
- BATTLES
- TEXAN MOVEMENTS
- MEXICAN MOVEMENTS

1 CONCEPCIÓN Oct. 1835
2 SAN ANTONIO Dec. 1835
3 THE ALAMO Mar. 1836

UNORGANIZED UNITED STATES TERRITORY

IOWA
MO.
ARK.

Arkansas R.
Texas–Mexico boundary as claimed by Texas
Boundary of Adams–Onis Treaty 1819
Red R.
Sabine R.
LA.

Area in dispute

TEXAS

Texas–Mexico boundary as claimed by Mexico

MEXICO

Rio Grande
Nueces R.

THE ALAMO

GULF OF MEXICO

SCALE OF MILES
0   100   200   300

© Copyright HAMMOND INCORPORATED, Maplewood, N.J.

UNITED STATES
ARKANSAS
LOUISIANA

T E X A S

Brazos R.
Trinity R.
Sabine R.
Red R.

Nacogdoches

Colorado R.
Austin
Washington
HOUSTON 1836
San Felipe de Austin 1836
SAN JACINTO Apr. 21, 1836

Guadalupe R.
Gonzales
SANTA ANNA 1835
GONZALES Oct. 2, 1835
Calveston Bay

San Antonio 1836
3 1835
2 1836
1 1836

FANNIN 1836
WARD 1836
Victoria
COLETO Mar. 1836
URREA 1836

SANTA ANNA 1836
Goliad
WARD 1836

Nueces R.
REFUGIO Mar. 1836
Refugio

San Patricio
SAN PATRICIO Feb. 1836
Agua Dulce

URREA 1836

GULF OF MEXICO

Matamoros   Brownsville

SCALE OF MILES
0   50   100   150

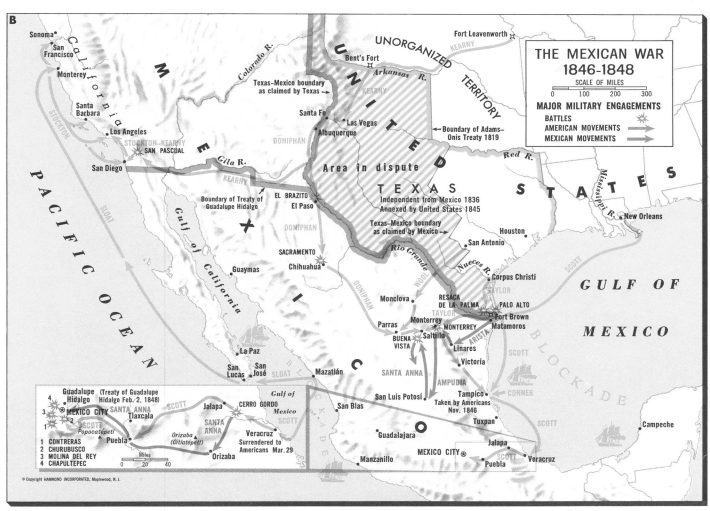

B — THE MEXICAN WAR 1846-1848

SCALE OF MILES
0   100   200   300

MAJOR MILITARY ENGAGEMENTS
- BATTLES
- AMERICAN MOVEMENTS
- MEXICAN MOVEMENTS

Sonoma
San Francisco
Monterey
Santa Barbara
Los Angeles
STOCKTON-KEARNY
SAN PASCUAL
San Diego
STOCKTON

PACIFIC OCEAN

California
MEXICO
Colorado R.
Gila R.
KEARNY

Fort Leavenworth
KEARNY
UNORGANIZED TERRITORY
Bent's Fort
Arkansas R.
KEARNY

Texas–Mexico boundary as claimed by Texas
Santa Fe
Las Vegas
Albuquerque
DONIPHAN

Boundary of Adams–Onis Treaty 1819
Area in dispute

UNITED STATES

Red R.
Mississippi R.
New Orleans

Boundary of Treaty of Guadalupe Hidalgo
EL BRAZITO
El Paso
DONIPHAN

SACRAMENTO
Chihuahua
Guaymas

TEXAS
Independent from Mexico 1836
Annexed by United States 1845
Texas–Mexico boundary as claimed by Mexico

Houston
San Antonio

Rio Grande
Nueces R.
Corpus Christi

DONIPHAN
Monclova
WOOL
Parras
Monterrey
MONTERREY
Saltillo
BUENA VISTA
ARISTA
RESACA DE LA PALMA
PALO ALTO
Fort Brown
Matamoros
TAYLOR

GULF OF MEXICO

BLOCKADE

Gulf of California
La Paz
San Lucas   San José
SLOAT
Mazatlán
SANTA ANNA
Linares
Victoria
AMPUDIA
Tampico Taken by Americans Nov. 1846
Tuxpan

San Luis Potosí
San Blas
Guadalajara
MEXICO CITY

Campeche
Jalapa
Veracruz
SCOTT
CONNER
BLOCKADE

Guadalupe Hidalgo (Treaty of Guadalupe Hidalgo Feb. 2, 1848)
SANTA ANNA
MEXICO CITY
Tlaxcala
Popocatépetl
Puebla
CERRO GORDO
Jalapa
SANTA ANNA
Orizaba (Citlatépetl)
Veracruz Surrendered to Americans Mar. 29
Orizaba
Gulf of Mexico
SCOTT

1 CONTRERAS
2 CHURUBUSCO
3 MOLINA DEL REY
4 CHAPULTEPEC

Miles
0   20   40

Manzanillo

© Copyright HAMMOND INCORPORATED, Maplewood, N.J.

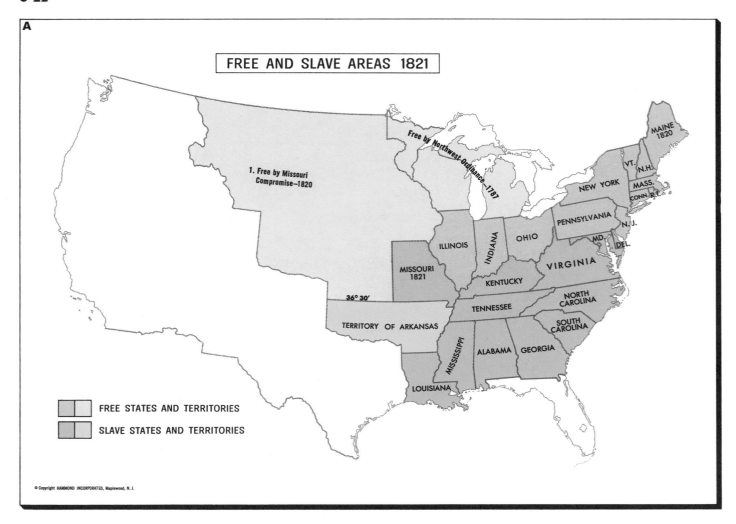

A

FREE AND SLAVE AREAS 1821

1. Free by Missouri Compromise—1820

Free by Northwest Ordinance—1787

MAINE 1820

VT. N.H.

NEW YORK

MASS. CONN. R.I.

PENNSYLVANIA

N.J.

MD. DEL.

ILLINOIS INDIANA OHIO

VIRGINIA

MISSOURI 1821

KENTUCKY

36° 30'

TENNESSEE

NORTH CAROLINA

TERRITORY OF ARKANSAS

SOUTH CAROLINA

MISSISSIPPI ALABAMA GEORGIA

LOUISIANA

FREE STATES AND TERRITORIES

SLAVE STATES AND TERRITORIES

© Copyright HAMMOND INCORPORATED, Maplewood, N.J.

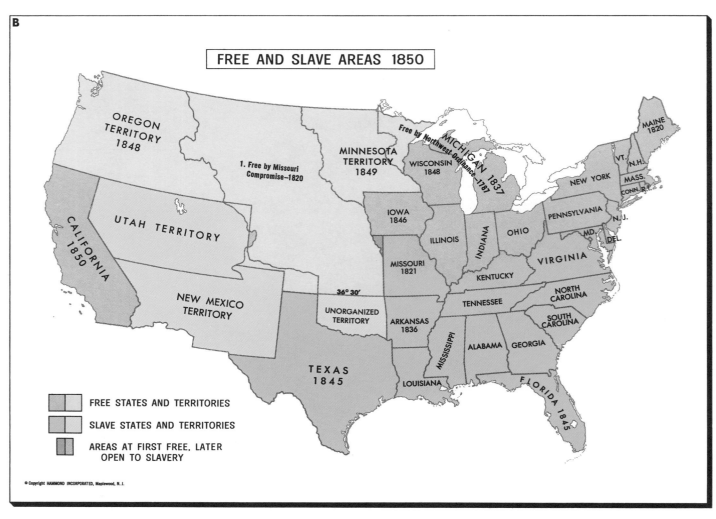

B

FREE AND SLAVE AREAS 1850

OREGON TERRITORY 1848

1. Free by Missouri Compromise—1820

MINNESOTA TERRITORY 1849

Free by Northwest Ordinance—1787

MICHIGAN 1837

WISCONSIN 1848

MAINE 1820

VT. N.H.

NEW YORK

MASS. CONN. R.I.

IOWA 1846

UTAH TERRITORY

CALIFORNIA 1850

ILLINOIS INDIANA OHIO

PENNSYLVANIA

N.J.

MD. DEL.

MISSOURI 1821

VIRGINIA

KENTUCKY

NEW MEXICO TERRITORY

36° 30'

TENNESSEE

NORTH CAROLINA

UNORGANIZED TERRITORY

ARKANSAS 1836

SOUTH CAROLINA

MISSISSIPPI ALABAMA GEORGIA

TEXAS 1845

LOUISIANA

FLORIDA 1845

FREE STATES AND TERRITORIES

SLAVE STATES AND TERRITORIES

AREAS AT FIRST FREE, LATER OPEN TO SLAVERY

© Copyright HAMMOND INCORPORATED, Maplewood, N.J.

C

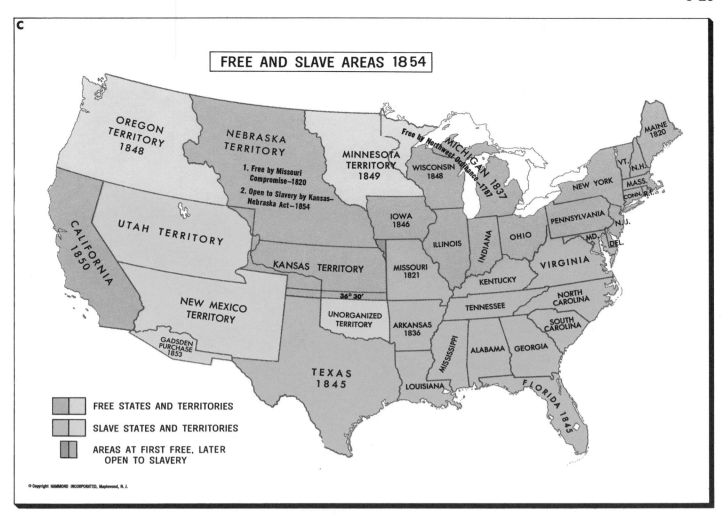

FREE AND SLAVE AREAS 1854

OREGON TERRITORY 1848

NEBRASKA TERRITORY

1. Free by Missouri Compromise—1820
2. Open to Slavery by Kansas–Nebraska Act—1854

MINNESOTA TERRITORY 1849

Free by Northwest Ordinance—1787

MICHIGAN 1837

WISCONSIN 1848

MAINE 1820

VT. N.H.

NEW YORK

MASS. CONN. R.I.

CALIFORNIA 1850

UTAH TERRITORY

IOWA 1846

ILLINOIS

INDIANA

OHIO

PENNSYLVANIA

N.J.

MD. DEL.

KANSAS TERRITORY

MISSOURI 1821

KENTUCKY

VIRGINIA

NEW MEXICO TERRITORY

36° 30'

UNORGANIZED TERRITORY

TENNESSEE

NORTH CAROLINA

GADSDEN PURCHASE 1853

ARKANSAS 1836

SOUTH CAROLINA

MISSISSIPPI

ALABAMA

GEORGIA

TEXAS 1845

LOUISIANA

FLORIDA 1845

FREE STATES AND TERRITORIES

SLAVE STATES AND TERRITORIES

AREAS AT FIRST FREE, LATER OPEN TO SLAVERY

D

FREE AND SLAVE AREAS 1861
at the outbreak of the Civil War

WASHINGTON TERRITORY

DAKOTA TERRITORY

MINNESOTA 1858

OREGON 1859

MICHIGAN

WISCONSIN

MAINE

VT. N.H.

NEW YORK

MASS. CONN. R.I.

NEVADA TERRITORY

UTAH TERRITORY

NEBRASKA TERRITORY

IOWA

CALIFORNIA

COLORADO TERRITORY

KANSAS 1861

ILLINOIS

INDIANA

OHIO

PENNSYLVANIA

N.J.

MASON-DIXON LINE

MD. DEL.

MISSOURI

PUBLIC LAND

INDIAN TERRITORY

KENTUCKY

VIRGINIA

NEW MEXICO TERRITORY

ARKANSAS

TENNESSEE

NORTH CAROLINA

SOUTH CAROLINA

MISSISSIPPI

ALABAMA

GEORGIA

TEXAS

LOUISIANA

FLORIDA

FREE STATES

SLAVE STATES

TERRITORIES OPEN TO SLAVERY BY DRED SCOTT DECISION 1857

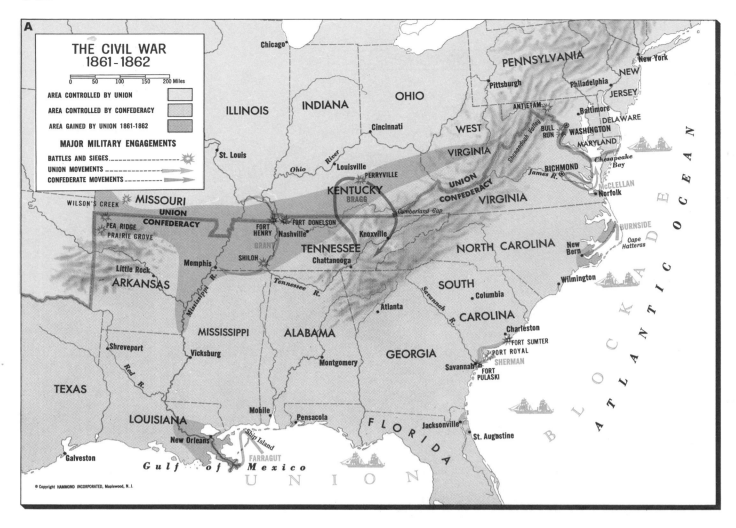

THE CIVIL WAR
1861-1862

0 50 100 150 200 Miles

AREA CONTROLLED BY UNION
AREA CONTROLLED BY CONFEDERACY
AREA GAINED BY UNION 1861-1862

MAJOR MILITARY ENGAGEMENTS

BATTLES AND SIEGES
UNION MOVEMENTS
CONFEDERATE MOVEMENTS

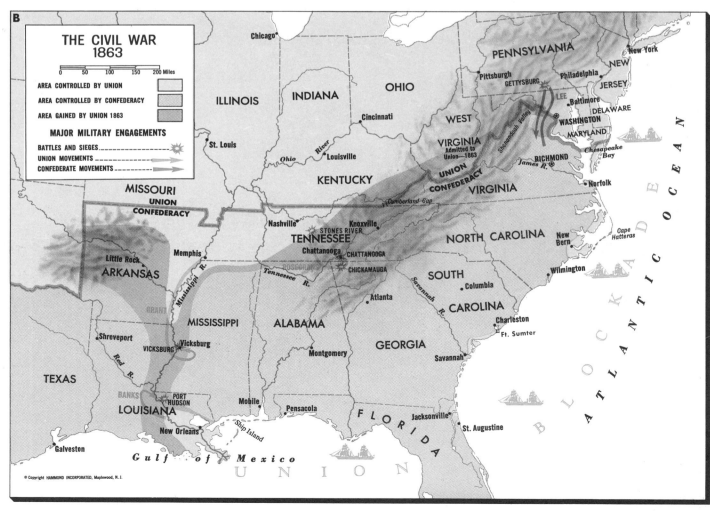

THE CIVIL WAR
1863

0 50 100 150 200 Miles

AREA CONTROLLED BY UNION
AREA CONTROLLED BY CONFEDERACY
AREA GAINED BY UNION 1863

MAJOR MILITARY ENGAGEMENTS

BATTLES AND SIEGES
UNION MOVEMENTS
CONFEDERATE MOVEMENTS

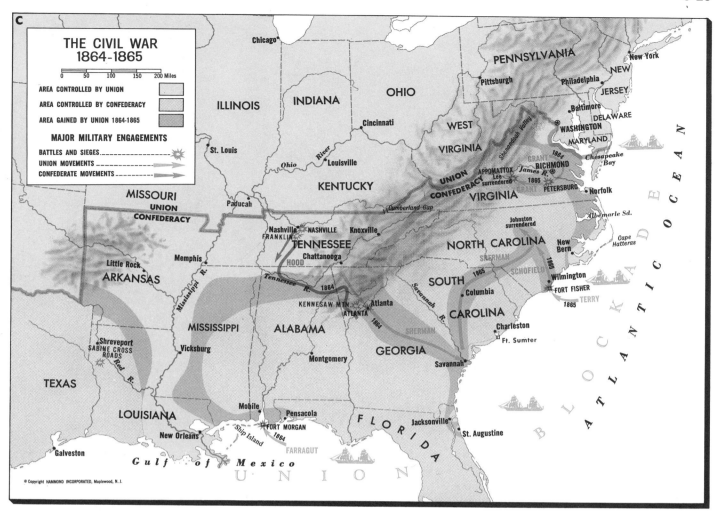

C

THE CIVIL WAR 1864-1865

0 50 100 150 200 Miles

AREA CONTROLLED BY UNION

AREA CONTROLLED BY CONFEDERACY

AREA GAINED BY UNION 1864-1865

MAJOR MILITARY ENGAGEMENTS

BATTLES AND SIEGES

UNION MOVEMENTS

CONFEDERATE MOVEMENTS

Chicago

New York

PENNSYLVANIA

NEW JERSEY

ILLINOIS

INDIANA

OHIO

Pittsburgh

Philadelphia

Baltimore

DELAWARE

WASHINGTON

MARYLAND

WEST VIRGINIA

Cincinnati

Shenandoah Valley

GRANT 1864

Chesapeake Bay

St. Louis

Ohio River

Louisville

KENTUCKY

UNION CONFEDERACY

APPOMATTOX Lee surrendered 1865

GRANT

RICHMOND

James R.

PETERSBURG

Norfolk

MISSOURI

UNION CONFEDERACY

Paducah

Cumberland Gap

VIRGINIA

Albemarle Sd.

Johnston surrendered

Nashville NASHVILLE FRANKLIN

Knoxville

NORTH CAROLINA

SHERMAN

New Bern

Cape Hatteras

Little Rock

Memphis

ARKANSAS

Chattanooga

HOOD

Tennessee R.

1864

SOUTH

SCHOFIELD

1865

Columbia

Wilmington

FORT FISHER

1865

TERRY

KENNESAW MTN

Atlanta

ATLANTA 1864

Savannah R.

CAROLINA

Charleston

Ft. Sumter

SHERMAN

MISSISSIPPI

ALABAMA

GEORGIA

Mississippi R.

Shreveport SABINE CROSS ROADS

Red R.

Vicksburg

Montgomery

Savannah

TEXAS

LOUISIANA

Mobile

Pensacola

Jacksonville

FLORIDA

St. Augustine

Galveston

New Orleans

Ship Island FORT MORGAN 1864

FARRAGUT

Gulf of Mexico

U N I O N

ATLANTIC OCEAN

BLOCKADE

© Copyright HAMMOND INCORPORATED, Maplewood, N.J.

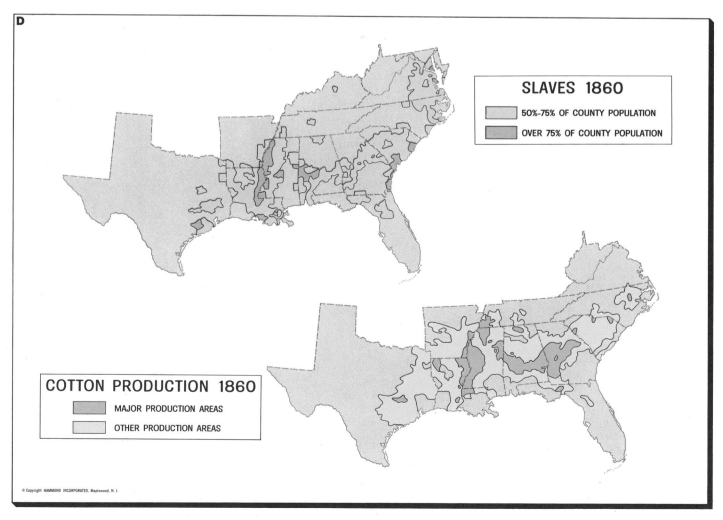

D

SLAVES 1860

50%-75% OF COUNTY POPULATION

OVER 75% OF COUNTY POPULATION

COTTON PRODUCTION 1860

MAJOR PRODUCTION AREAS

OTHER PRODUCTION AREAS

© Copyright HAMMOND INCORPORATED, Maplewood, N.J.

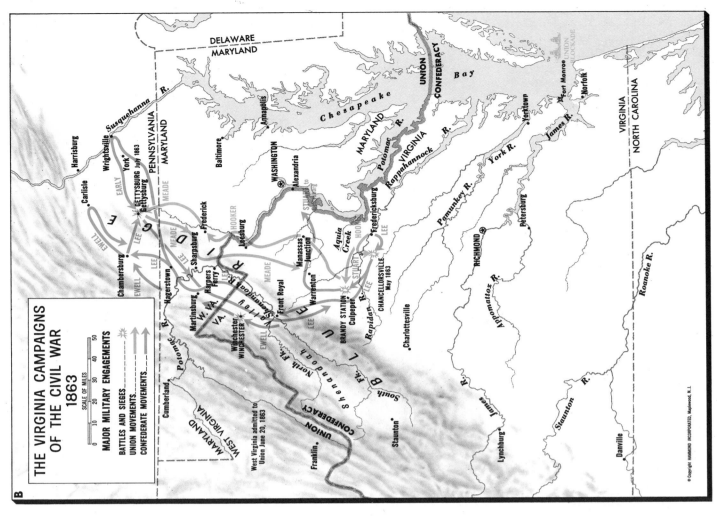

THE VIRGINIA CAMPAIGNS
OF THE CIVIL WAR
1863

SCALE OF MILES
0 10 20 30 40 50

MAJOR MILITARY ENGAGEMENTS

BATTLES AND SIEGES
UNION MOVEMENTS
CONFEDERATE MOVEMENTS

West Virginia admitted to
Union June 20, 1863

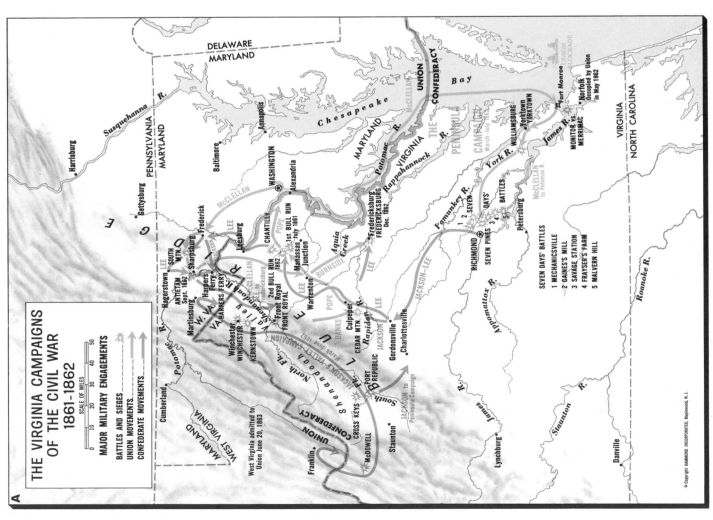

THE VIRGINIA CAMPAIGNS
OF THE CIVIL WAR
1861-1862

SCALE OF MILES
0 10 20 30 40 50

MAJOR MILITARY ENGAGEMENTS

BATTLES AND SIEGES
UNION MOVEMENTS
CONFEDERATE MOVEMENTS

West Virginia admitted to
Union June 20, 1863

SEVEN DAYS' BATTLES
1 MECHANICSVILLE
2 GAINES'S MILL
3 SAVAGE STATION
4 FRAYSER'S FARM
5 MALVERN HILL

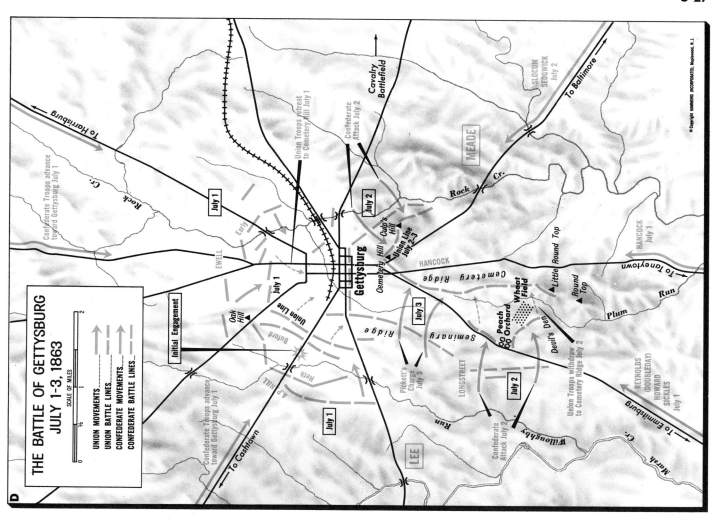

THE BATTLE OF GETTYSBURG
JULY 1-3, 1863

SCALE OF MILES

UNION MOVEMENTS
UNION BATTLE LINES
CONFEDERATE MOVEMENTS
CONFEDERATE BATTLE LINES

Confederate Troops advance toward Gettysburg July 1

To Harrisburg

Cr.

Rock

July 1

Early

EWELL

Oak Hill

July 1

Buford

Union Line

Heth

July 1

A.P. HILL

July 1

To Cashtown

LEE

Seminary Ridge

Pickett's Charge July 3

July 3

Longstreet

July 2

Confederate Attack July 2

Willoughby

Run

Mar'sh

Cr.

Confederate Troops advance toward Gettysburg July 1

Union Troops retreat to Cemetery Hill July 1

Gettysburg

Cemetery Hill

Culp's Hill

Union Line July 2-3

July 2

Confederate Attack July 2

Cavalry Battlefield

To Baltimore

SLOCUM

SEDGWICK

July 2

MEADE

Rock Cr.

HANCOCK

Cemetery Ridge

Little Round Top

July 2

Round Top

Peach Orchard

Wheat Field

Devil's Den

Union Troops withdraw to Cemetery Ridge July 2

Plum

Run

HANCOCK July 1

To Taneytown

REYNOLDS (DOUBLEDAY)
HOWARD
SICKLES

July 1

To Emmitsburg

Initial Engagement

© Copyright HAMMOND INCORPORATED, Maplewood, N.J.

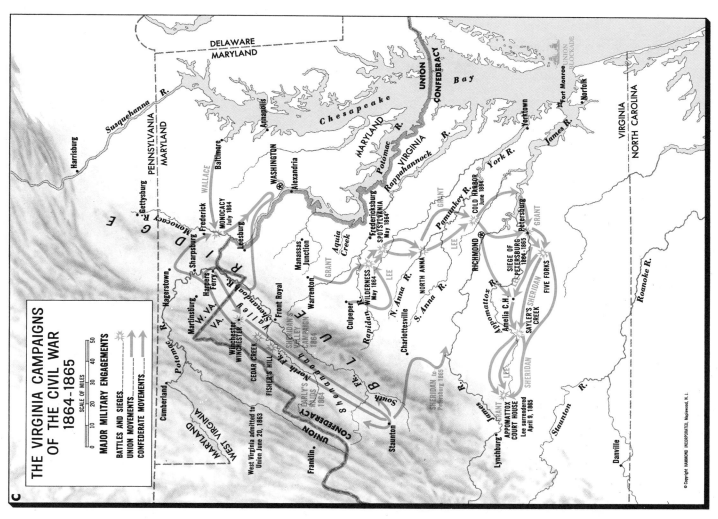

THE VIRGINIA CAMPAIGNS
OF THE CIVIL WAR
1864-1865

SCALE OF MILES
0 10 20 30 40 50

MAJOR MILITARY ENGAGEMENTS

BATTLES AND SIEGES
UNION MOVEMENTS
CONFEDERATE MOVEMENTS

West Virginia admitted to Union June 20, 1863

PENNSYLVANIA
MARYLAND

DELAWARE
MARYLAND

Susquehanna R.

Harrisburg

RIDGE

Gettysburg

Monocacy R.

Sharpsburg

Hagerstown

Martinsburg

Cumberland

Potomac R.

W. VA.

VA.

Harpers Ferry

Winchester
WINCHESTER

CEDAR CREEK

FISHER'S HILL

EARLY'S RAIDS 1864

North Fk.

SHERIDAN'S VALLEY CAMPAIGN 1864

Shenandoah

South Fk.

Valley

Staunton

Staunton R.

Lynchburg

APPOMATTOX COURT HOUSE
Lee surrendered April 9, 1865

Danville

Franklin

MARYLAND
WEST VIRGINIA

UNION
CONFEDERACY

Frederick

MONOCACY
July 1864

WALLACE

Leesburg

Front Royal

Warrenton

Manassas Junction

Culpeper

Rapidan R.

Aquia Creek

Rappahannock R.

Fredericksburg
SPOTSYLVANIA
May 1864

WILDERNESS
May 1864

N. Anna R.

NORTH ANNA

S. Anna R.

Charlottesville

GRANT

LEE

Pamunkey R.

COLD HARBOR
June 1864

RICHMOND

SIEGE OF PETERSBURG
1864-1865

Petersburg

GRANT

Appomattox R.

Amelia C.H.

SAYLER'S CREEK

FIVE FORKS

SHERIDAN

LEE

GRANT

SHERIDAN to Petersburg 1865

Juni R.

Roanoke R.

WASHINGTON

Alexandria

Annapolis

Baltimore

MARYLAND

Potomac R.

VIRGINIA

Chesapeake

Bay

UNION BLOCKADE

Fort Monroe

Yorktown

Norfolk

York R.

James R.

VIRGINIA
NORTH CAROLINA

UNION
CONFEDERACY

© Copyright HAMMOND INCORPORATED, Maplewood, N.J.

A

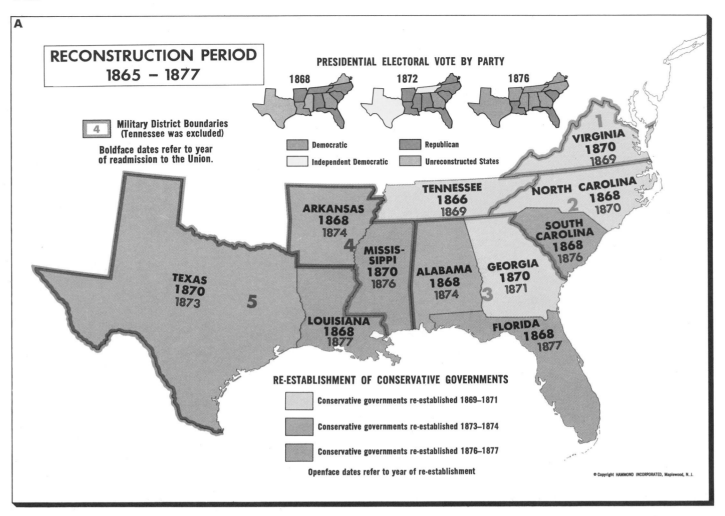

RECONSTRUCTION PERIOD 1865 – 1877

PRESIDENTIAL ELECTORAL VOTE BY PARTY

1868   1872   1876

Democratic   Republican

Independent Democratic   Unreconstructed States

[4] Military District Boundaries (Tennessee was excluded)

Boldface dates refer to year of readmission to the Union.

VIRGINIA 1870 *1869*

TENNESSEE 1866 *1869*

NORTH CAROLINA 1868 *1870*

ARKANSAS 1868 *1874*

SOUTH CAROLINA 1868 *1876*

MISSISSIPPI 1870 *1876*

ALABAMA 1868 *1874*

GEORGIA 1870 *1871*

TEXAS 1870 *1873*

LOUISIANA 1868 *1877*

FLORIDA 1868 *1877*

RE-ESTABLISHMENT OF CONSERVATIVE GOVERNMENTS

Conservative governments re-established 1869–1871

Conservative governments re-established 1873–1874

Conservative governments re-established 1876–1877

Openface dates refer to year of re-establishment

© Copyright HAMMOND INCORPORATED, Maplewood, N.J.

B

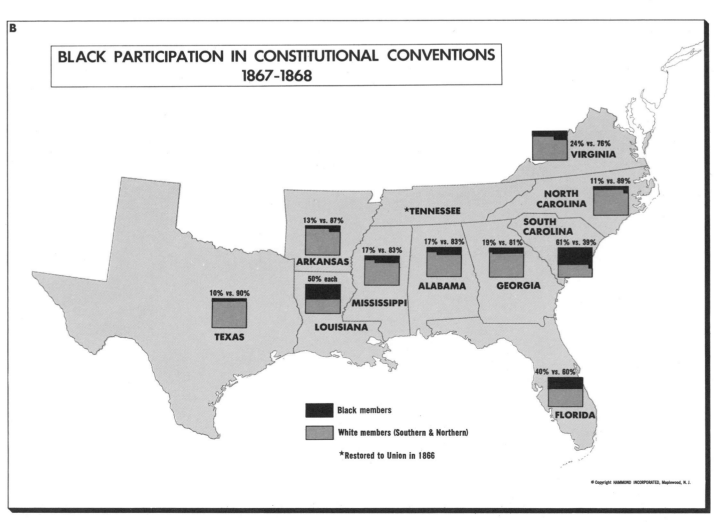

BLACK PARTICIPATION IN CONSTITUTIONAL CONVENTIONS 1867-1868

24% vs. 76% VIRGINIA

11% vs. 89% NORTH CAROLINA

*TENNESSEE

SOUTH CAROLINA

13% vs. 87% ARKANSAS

17% vs. 83% MISSISSIPPI

17% vs. 83% ALABAMA

19% vs. 81% GEORGIA

61% vs. 39%

50% each

10% vs. 90% TEXAS

LOUISIANA

40% vs. 60% FLORIDA

Black members

White members (Southern & Northern)

*Restored to Union in 1866

© Copyright HAMMOND INCORPORATED, Maplewood, N.J.

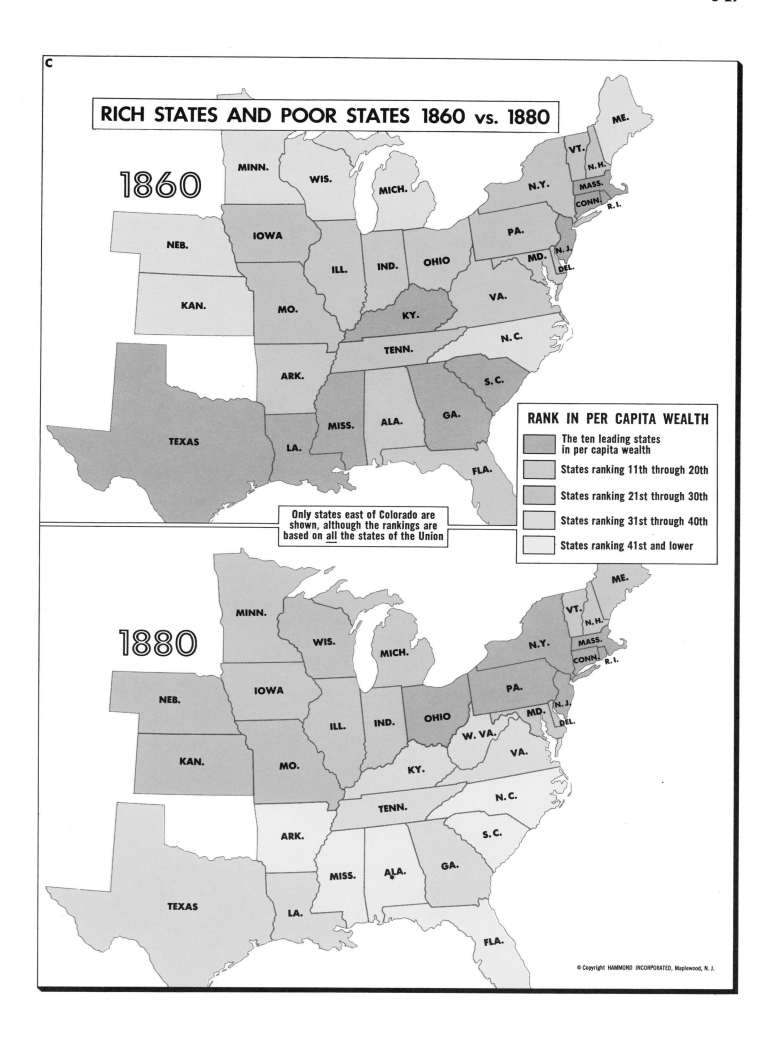

RICH STATES AND POOR STATES 1860 vs. 1880

1860

1880

Only states east of Colorado are shown, although the rankings are based on all the states of the Union

RANK IN PER CAPITA WEALTH

The ten leading states in per capita wealth

States ranking 11th through 20th

States ranking 21st through 30th

States ranking 31st through 40th

States ranking 41st and lower

© Copyright HAMMOND INCORPORATED, Maplewood, N. J.

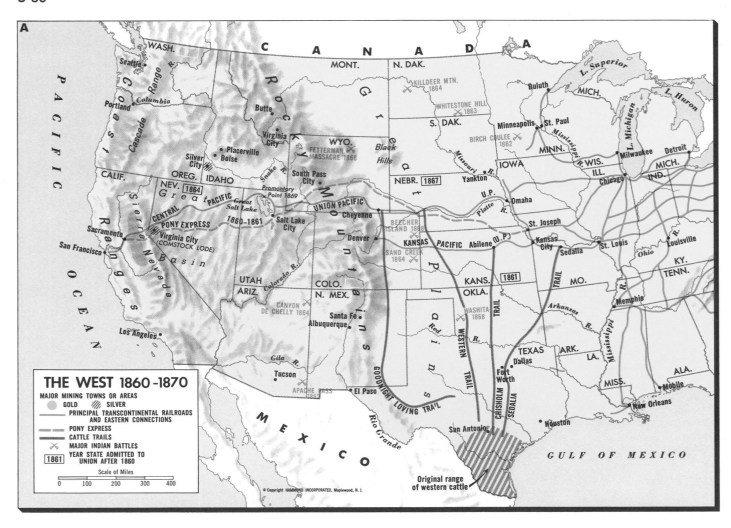

A

THE WEST 1860-1870

MAJOR MINING TOWNS OR AREAS

- ● GOLD ▨ SILVER
- ── PRINCIPAL TRANSCONTINENTAL RAILROADS AND EASTERN CONNECTIONS
- ─ ─ PONY EXPRESS
- ── CATTLE TRAILS
- ✕ MAJOR INDIAN BATTLES
- ☐1861 YEAR STATE ADMITTED TO UNION AFTER 1860

Scale of Miles
0   100   200   300   400

© Copyright HAMMOND INCORPORATED, Maplewood, N.J.

Original range of western cattle

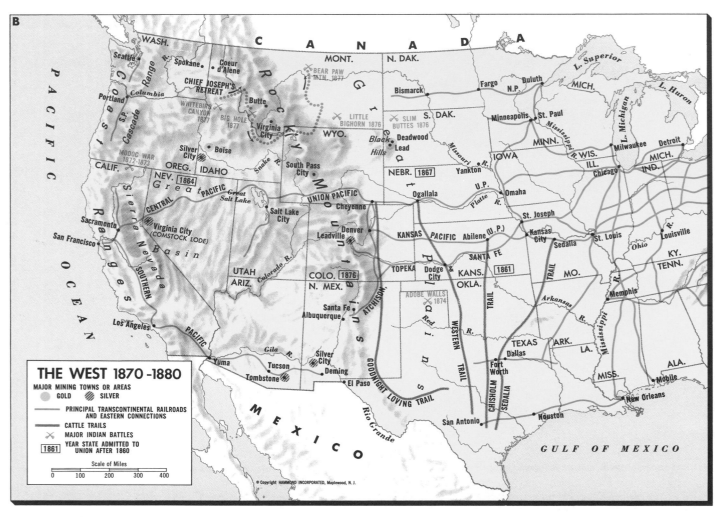

B

THE WEST 1870-1880

MAJOR MINING TOWNS OR AREAS

- ● GOLD ▨ SILVER
- ── PRINCIPAL TRANSCONTINENTAL RAILROADS AND EASTERN CONNECTIONS
- ── CATTLE TRAILS
- ✕ MAJOR INDIAN BATTLES
- ☐1861 YEAR STATE ADMITTED TO UNION AFTER 1860

Scale of Miles
0   100   200   300   400

© Copyright HAMMOND INCORPORATED, Maplewood, N.J.

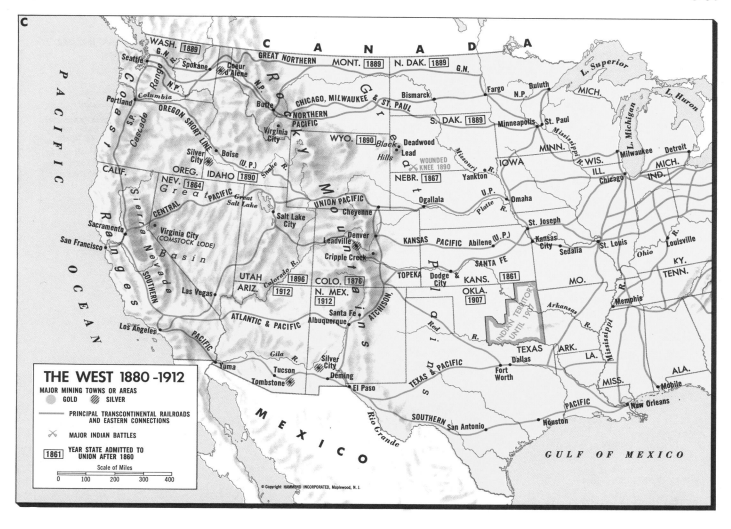

THE WEST 1880-1912

MAJOR MINING TOWNS OR AREAS
- ● GOLD
- ◨ SILVER

— PRINCIPAL TRANSCONTINENTAL RAILROADS AND EASTERN CONNECTIONS

✕ MAJOR INDIAN BATTLES

1861 YEAR STATE ADMITTED TO UNION AFTER 1860

Scale of Miles
0   100   200   300   400

© Copyright HAMMOND INCORPORATED, Maplewood, N.J.

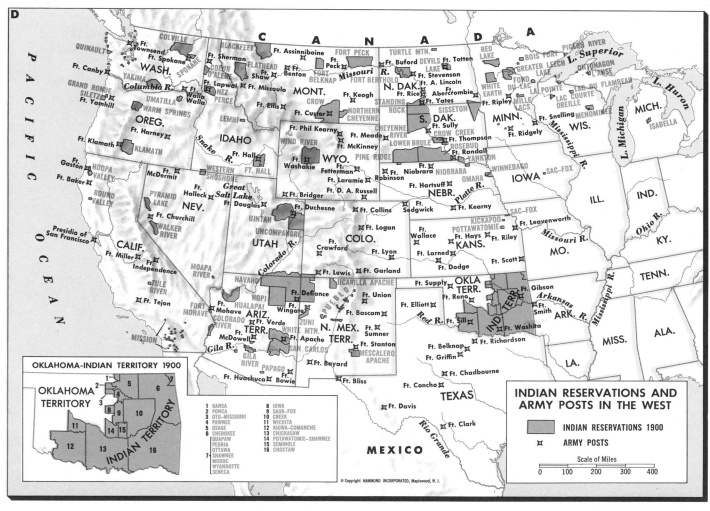

OKLAHOMA-INDIAN TERRITORY 1900

OKLAHOMA TERRITORY

INDIAN TERRITORY

1 KANSA
2 PONCA
3 OTO–MISSOURI
4 PAWNEE
5 OSAGE
6 CHEROKEE
  QUAPAW
  PEORIA
  OTTAWA
7 SHAWNEE
  MODOC
  WYANDOTTE
  SENECA
8 IOWA
9 SAUK–FOX
10 CREEK
11 WICHITA
12 KIOWA–COMANCHE
13 CHICKASAW
14 POTAWATOMIE–SHAWNEE
15 SEMINOLE
16 CHOCTAW

INDIAN RESERVATIONS AND ARMY POSTS IN THE WEST

▨ INDIAN RESERVATIONS 1900
⚔ ARMY POSTS

Scale of Miles
0   100   200   300   400

© Copyright HAMMOND INCORPORATED, Maplewood, N.J.

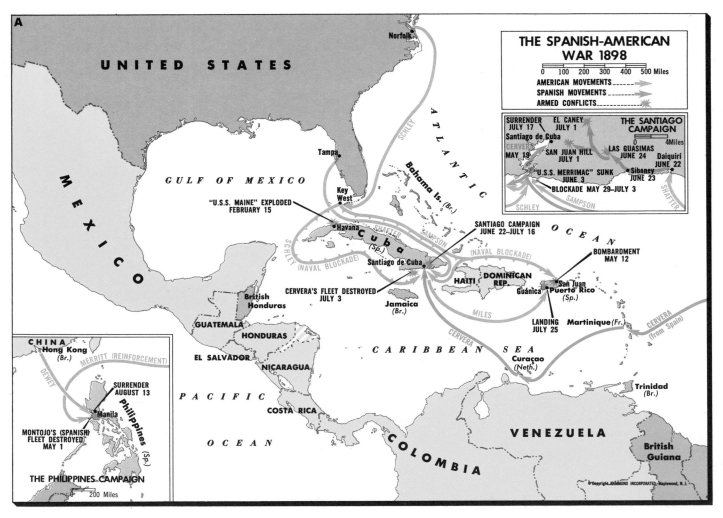

A

UNITED STATES

GULF OF MEXICO

MEXICO

Norfolk

THE SPANISH-AMERICAN
WAR 1898

0   100   200   300   400   500 Miles

AMERICAN MOVEMENTS ------→
SPANISH MOVEMENTS ------→
ARMED CONFLICTS ------ ✳

THE SANTIAGO
CAMPAIGN

SURRENDER   EL CANEY
JULY 17   JULY 1
Santiago de Cuba   0   4 Miles
CERVERA   LAS GUASIMAS
MAY 19   SAN JUAN HILL   JUNE 24
         JULY 1   Daiquirí
"U.S.S. MERRIMAC" SUNK   Siboney   JUNE 22
JUNE 3   JUNE 23
BLOCKADE MAY 29–JULY 3

Tampa

Bahama Is.
(Br.)

Key
West

"U.S.S. MAINE" EXPLODED
FEBRUARY 15

Havana

SCHLEY (NAVAL BLOCKADE)

Cuba
(Sp.)

SANTIAGO CAMPAIGN
JUNE 22–JULY 16

SANTIAGO

(NAVAL BLOCKADE)

BOMBARDMENT
MAY 12

Santiago de Cuba

CERVERA'S FLEET DESTROYED
JULY 3

HAITI   DOMINICAN
        REP.

San Juan
Guánica   Puerto Rico
          (Sp.)

Jamaica
(Br.)

MILES

CERVERA
(from Spain)

LANDING
JULY 25   Martinique (Fr.)

British
Honduras

GUATEMALA

HONDURAS

EL SALVADOR

NICARAGUA

CHINA
Hong Kong
(Br.)

MERRITT (REINFORCEMENT)

DEWEY

SURRENDER
AUGUST 13
Manila

Philippines
(Sp.)

MONTOJO'S (SPANISH)
FLEET DESTROYED
MAY 1

THE PHILIPPINES CAMPAIGN

200 Miles

PACIFIC

OCEAN

COSTA RICA

CARIBBEAN   SEA

Curaçao
(Neth.)

VENEZUELA

COLOMBIA

Trinidad
(Br.)

British
Guiana

© Copyright HAMMOND INCORPORATED, Maplewood, N.J.

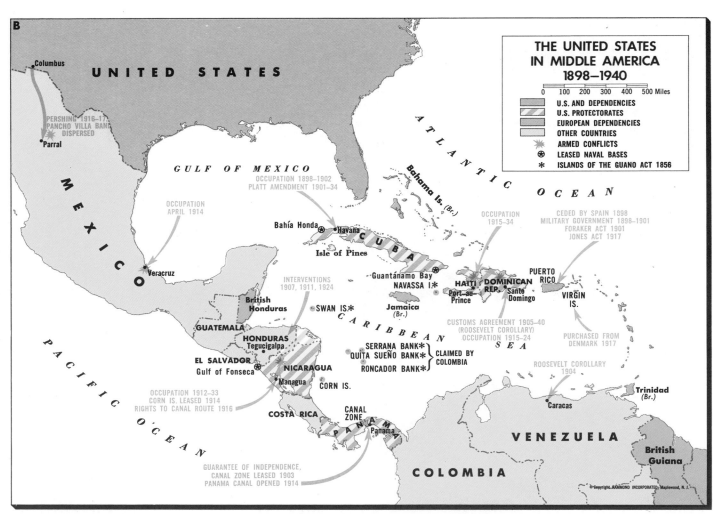

B

Columbus

UNITED   STATES

PERSHING 1916–17
PANCHO VILLA BAND
DISPERSED
Parral

MEXICO

THE UNITED STATES
IN MIDDLE AMERICA
1898–1940

0   100   200   300   400   500 Miles

☐ U.S. AND DEPENDENCIES
☐ U.S. PROTECTORATES
☐ EUROPEAN DEPENDENCIES
☐ OTHER COUNTRIES
✳ ARMED CONFLICTS
⊗ LEASED NAVAL BASES
✳ ISLANDS OF THE GUANO ACT 1856

GULF OF MEXICO

OCCUPATION 1898–1902
PLATT AMENDMENT 1901–34

OCCUPATION
APRIL 1914

Veracruz

Bahía Honda   Havana
Isle of Pines

British
Honduras

GUATEMALA

INTERVENTIONS
1907, 1911, 1924

CUBA

OCCUPATION
1915–34

Guantánamo Bay
NAVASSA I ✳

Jamaica
(Br.)

HAITI   DOMINICAN
Port-au-   REP.
Prince   Santo
           Domingo

CEDED BY SPAIN 1898
MILITARY GOVERNMENT 1898–1901
FORAKER ACT 1901
JONES ACT 1917

PUERTO
RICO

VIRGIN
IS.

PURCHASED FROM
DENMARK 1917

HONDURAS
Tegucigalpa

EL SALVADOR
Gulf of Fonseca

NICARAGUA
Managua

OCCUPATION 1912–33
CORN IS. LEASED 1914
RIGHTS TO CANAL ROUTE 1916

COSTA RICA

CARIBBEAN

SWAN IS ✳

SERRANA BANK ✳
QUITA SUEÑO BANK ✳
RONCADOR BANK ✳

CORN IS.

CLAIMED BY
COLOMBIA

CUSTOMS AGREEMENT 1905–40
(ROOSEVELT COROLLARY)
OCCUPATION 1915–24

SEA

ROOSEVELT COROLLARY
1904

ATLANTIC   OCEAN

PACIFIC   OCEAN

CANAL
ZONE
PANAMA
Panama

GUARANTEE OF INDEPENDENCE,
CANAL ZONE LEASED 1903
PANAMA CANAL OPENED 1914

COLOMBIA

Caracas

VENEZUELA

Trinidad
(Br.)

British
Guiana

© Copyright HAMMOND INCORPORATED, Maplewood, N.J.

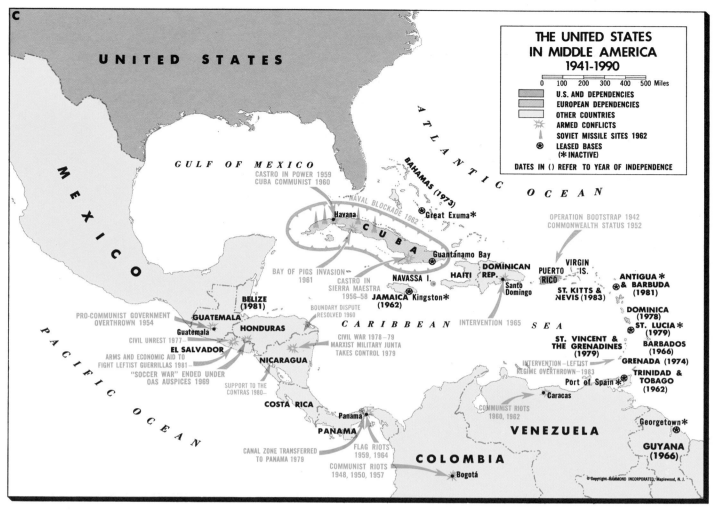

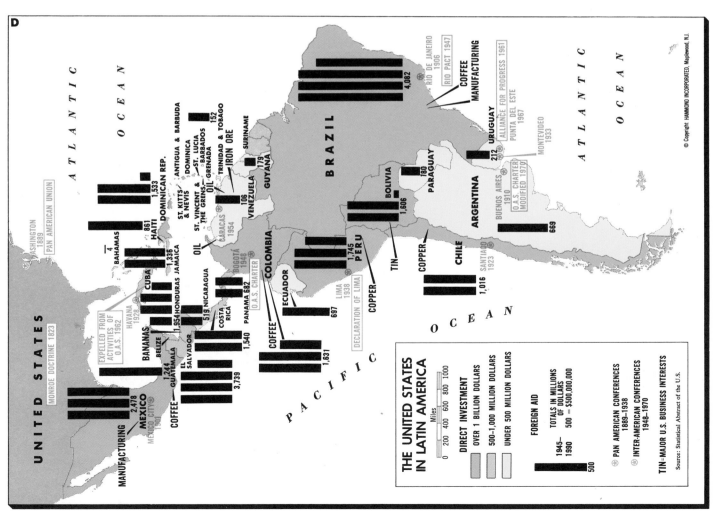

A

GROWTH OF INDUSTRY AND CITIES 1860

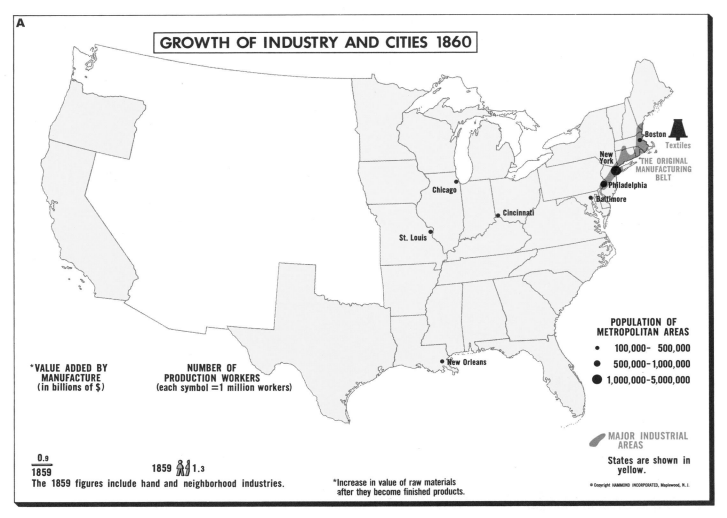

Boston
Textiles

New York
THE ORIGINAL MANUFACTURING BELT

Chicago

Philadelphia

Baltimore

Cincinnati

St. Louis

New Orleans

POPULATION OF METROPOLITAN AREAS
- · 100,000- 500,000
- ● 500,000-1,000,000
- ● 1,000,000-5,000,000

*VALUE ADDED BY MANUFACTURE (in billions of $)

NUMBER OF PRODUCTION WORKERS (each symbol = 1 million workers)

0.9 / 1859

1859 🧍🧍 1.3

The 1859 figures include hand and neighborhood industries.

*Increase in value of raw materials after they become finished products.

MAJOR INDUSTRIAL AREAS

States are shown in yellow.

© Copyright HAMMOND INCORPORATED, Maplewood, N. J.

B

GROWTH OF INDUSTRY AND CITIES 1900

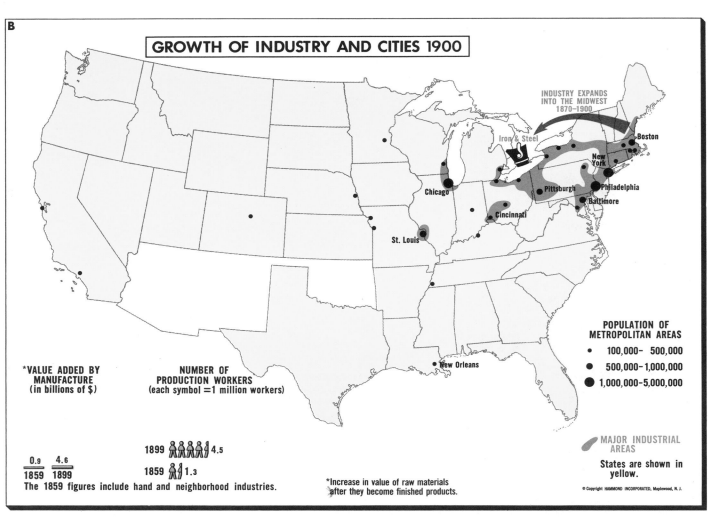

INDUSTRY EXPANDS INTO THE MIDWEST 1870–1900

Iron & Steel

Boston

New York

Chicago

Pittsburgh

Philadelphia

Baltimore

Cincinnati

St. Louis

New Orleans

POPULATION OF METROPOLITAN AREAS
- · 100,000- 500,000
- ● 500,000-1,000,000
- ● 1,000,000-5,000,000

*VALUE ADDED BY MANUFACTURE (in billions of $)

NUMBER OF PRODUCTION WORKERS (each symbol = 1 million workers)

1899 🧍🧍🧍🧍🧍 4.5

0.9 / 1859   4.6 / 1899

1859 🧍🧍 1.3

The 1859 figures include hand and neighborhood industries.

*Increase in value of raw materials after they become finished products.

MAJOR INDUSTRIAL AREAS

States are shown in yellow.

© Copyright HAMMOND INCORPORATED, Maplewood, N. J.

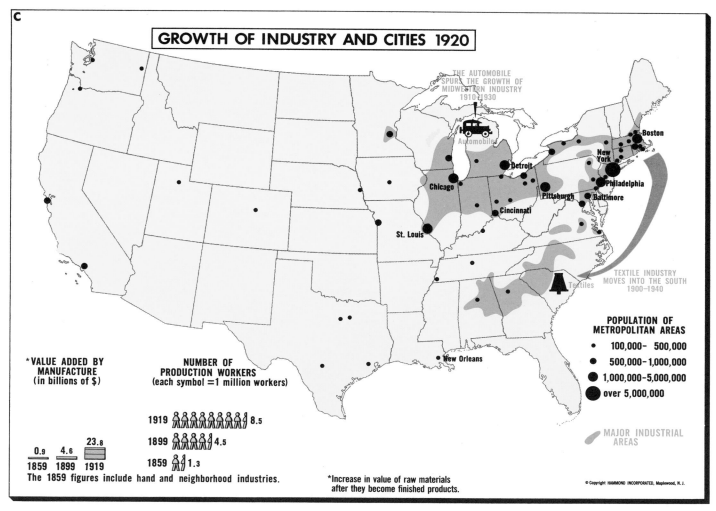

GROWTH OF INDUSTRY AND CITIES 1920

THE AUTOMOBILE SPURS THE GROWTH OF MIDWESTERN INDUSTRY 1910-1930

Automobiles

TEXTILE INDUSTRY MOVES INTO THE SOUTH 1900-1940

Textiles

POPULATION OF METROPOLITAN AREAS
- 100,000– 500,000
- 500,000–1,000,000
- 1,000,000–5,000,000
- over 5,000,000

MAJOR INDUSTRIAL AREAS

*VALUE ADDED BY MANUFACTURE (in billions of $)

NUMBER OF PRODUCTION WORKERS (each symbol =1 million workers)

1919 8.5
1899 4.5
1859 1.3

0.9 / 4.6 / 23.8
1859 / 1899 / 1919

The 1859 figures include hand and neighborhood industries.

*Increase in value of raw materials after they become finished products.

© Copyright HAMMOND INCORPORATED, Maplewood, N.J.

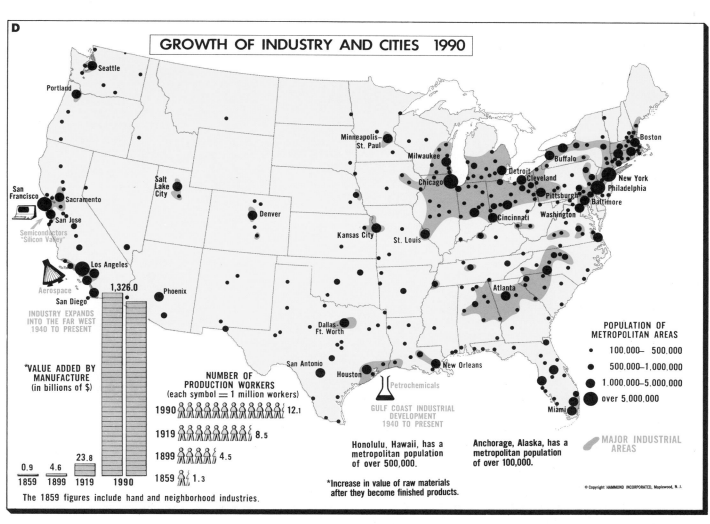

GROWTH OF INDUSTRY AND CITIES 1990

Semiconductors "Silicon Valley"

Aerospace

INDUSTRY EXPANDS INTO THE FAR WEST 1940 TO PRESENT

*VALUE ADDED BY MANUFACTURE (in billions of $)

1,326.0

NUMBER OF PRODUCTION WORKERS (each symbol = 1 million workers)

1990 12.1
1919 8.5
1899 4.5
1859 1.3

0.9 / 4.6 / 23.8 /
1859 / 1899 / 1919 / 1990

The 1859 figures include hand and neighborhood industries.

Petrochemicals

GULF COAST INDUSTRIAL DEVELOPMENT 1940 TO PRESENT

Honolulu, Hawaii, has a metropolitan population of over 500,000.

Anchorage, Alaska, has a metropolitan population of over 100,000.

*Increase in value of raw materials after they become finished products.

POPULATION OF METROPOLITAN AREAS
- 100,000– 500,000
- 500,000–1,000,000
- 1,000,000–5,000,000
- over 5,000,000

MAJOR INDUSTRIAL AREAS

© Copyright HAMMOND INCORPORATED, Maplewood, N.J.

A

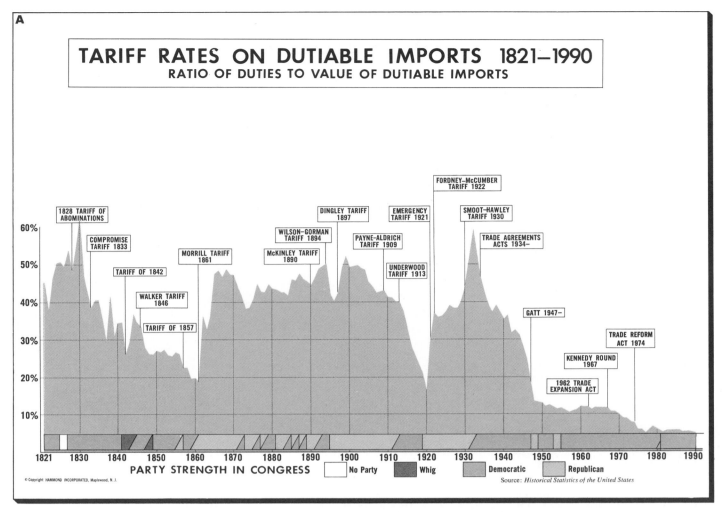

TARIFF RATES ON DUTIABLE IMPORTS 1821–1990
RATIO OF DUTIES TO VALUE OF DUTIABLE IMPORTS

FORDNEY–McCUMBER TARIFF 1922

1828 TARIFF OF ABOMINATIONS

COMPROMISE TARIFF 1833

TARIFF OF 1842

WALKER TARIFF 1846

TARIFF OF 1857

MORRILL TARIFF 1861

McKINLEY TARIFF 1890

WILSON–GORMAN TARIFF 1894

DINGLEY TARIFF 1897

PAYNE–ALDRICH TARIFF 1909

UNDERWOOD TARIFF 1913

EMERGENCY TARIFF 1921

SMOOT–HAWLEY TARIFF 1930

TRADE AGREEMENTS ACTS 1934–

GATT 1947–

KENNEDY ROUND 1967

1962 TRADE EXPANSION ACT

TRADE REFORM ACT 1974

PARTY STRENGTH IN CONGRESS — No Party — Whig — Democratic — Republican

1821 1830 1840 1850 1860 1870 1880 1890 1900 1910 1920 1930 1940 1950 1960 1970 1980 1990

60% 50% 40% 30% 20% 10%

© Copyright HAMMOND INCORPORATED, Maplewood, N.J.

Source: *Historical Statistics of the United States*

B

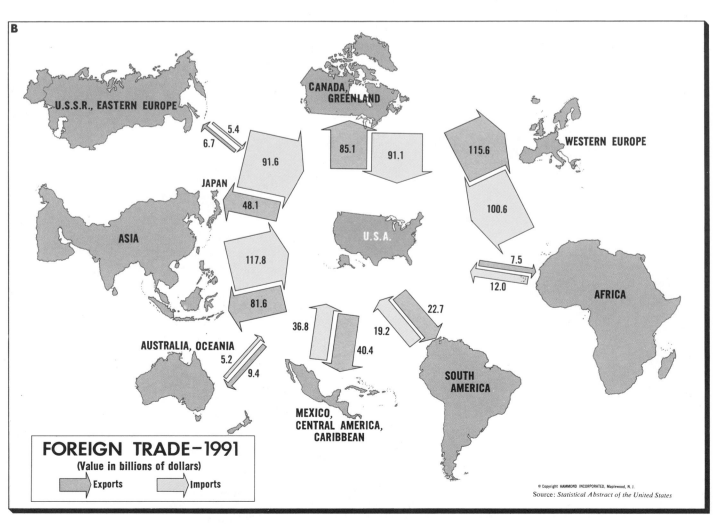

U.S.S.R., EASTERN EUROPE — 5.4 / 6.7

CANADA, GREENLAND — 85.1 / 91.1

WESTERN EUROPE — 115.6 / 100.6

JAPAN — 91.6 / 48.1

ASIA — 117.8 / 81.6

AUSTRALIA, OCEANIA — 5.2 / 9.4

MEXICO, CENTRAL AMERICA, CARIBBEAN — 36.8 / 40.4

SOUTH AMERICA — 22.7 / 19.2

AFRICA — 7.5 / 12.0

U.S.A.

FOREIGN TRADE–1991
(Value in billions of dollars)
— Exports — Imports

© Copyright HAMMOND INCORPORATED, Maplewood, N.J.

Source: *Statistical Abstract of the United States*

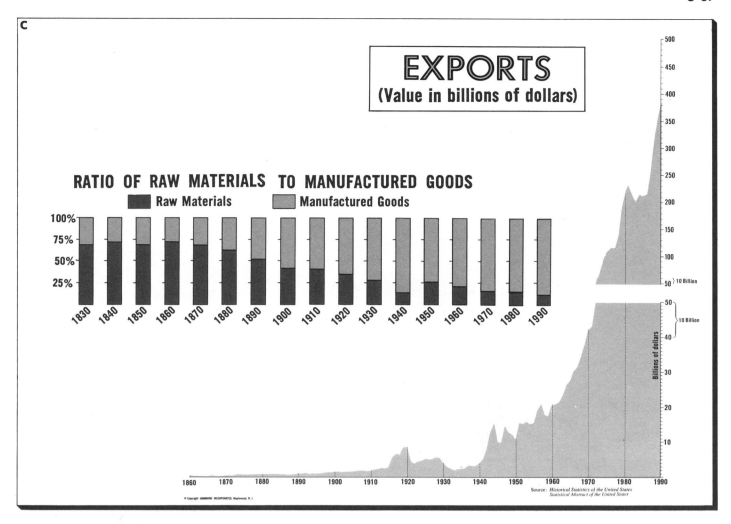

EXPORTS
(Value in billions of dollars)

RATIO OF RAW MATERIALS TO MANUFACTURED GOODS
Raw Materials   Manufactured Goods

Source: *Historical Statistics of the United States*
Statistical Abstract of the United States

© Copyright HAMMOND INCORPORATED, Maplewood, N. J.

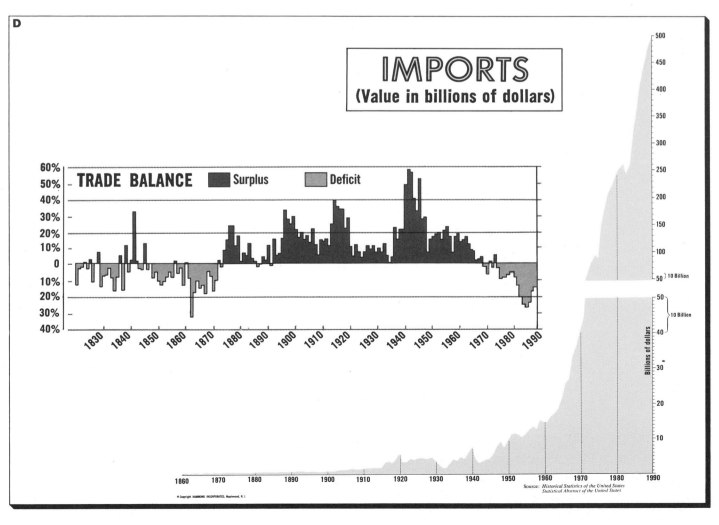

IMPORTS
(Value in billions of dollars)

TRADE BALANCE   Surplus   Deficit

Source: *Historical Statistics of the United States*
Statistical Abstract of the United States

© Copyright HAMMOND INCORPORATED, Maplewood, N. J.

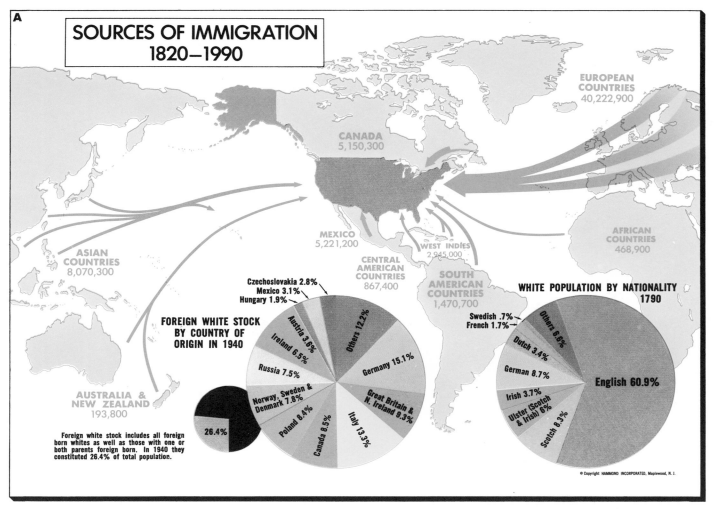

A

SOURCES OF IMMIGRATION 1820–1990

EUROPEAN COUNTRIES 40,222,900

CANADA 5,150,300

ASIAN COUNTRIES 8,070,300

MEXICO 5,221,200

CENTRAL AMERICAN COUNTRIES 867,400

WEST INDIES 2,945,000

SOUTH AMERICAN COUNTRIES 1,470,700

AFRICAN COUNTRIES 468,900

AUSTRALIA & NEW ZEALAND 193,800

FOREIGN WHITE STOCK BY COUNTRY OF ORIGIN IN 1940

- Czechoslovakia 2.8%
- Mexico 3.1%
- Hungary 1.9%
- Austria 3.6%
- Ireland 6.5%
- Russia 7.5%
- Norway, Sweden & Denmark 7.8%
- Poland 8.4%
- Canada 8.5%
- Italy 13.3%
- Great Britain & N. Ireland 9.3%
- Germany 15.1%
- Others 12.2%

26.4%

Foreign white stock includes all foreign born whites as well as those with one or both parents foreign born. In 1940 they constituted 26.4% of total population.

WHITE POPULATION BY NATIONALITY 1790

- Swedish .7%
- French 1.7%
- Dutch 3.4%
- German 8.7%
- Irish 3.7%
- Ulster (Scotch & Irish) 6%
- Scotch 8.3%
- English 60.9%
- Others 6.6%

© Copyright HAMMOND INCORPORATED, Maplewood, N.J.

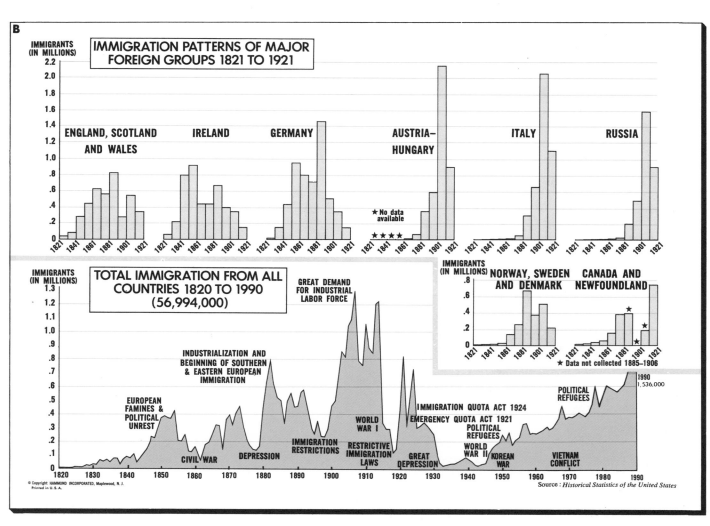

B

IMMIGRATION PATTERNS OF MAJOR FOREIGN GROUPS 1821 TO 1921

IMMIGRANTS (IN MILLIONS)

ENGLAND, SCOTLAND AND WALES

IRELAND

GERMANY

AUSTRIA–HUNGARY

★ No data available

★ ★ ★ ★

ITALY

RUSSIA

1821 1841 1861 1881 1901 1921

TOTAL IMMIGRATION FROM ALL COUNTRIES 1820 TO 1990 (56,994,000)

IMMIGRANTS (IN MILLIONS)

GREAT DEMAND FOR INDUSTRIAL LABOR FORCE

INDUSTRIALIZATION AND BEGINNING OF SOUTHERN & EASTERN EUROPEAN IMMIGRATION

EUROPEAN FAMINES & POLITICAL UNREST

CIVIL WAR

DEPRESSION

IMMIGRATION RESTRICTIONS

RESTRICTIVE IMMIGRATION LAWS

WORLD WAR I

IMMIGRATION QUOTA ACT 1924

EMERGENCY QUOTA ACT 1921

POLITICAL REFUGEES

GREAT DEPRESSION

WORLD WAR II

KOREAN WAR

VIETNAM CONFLICT

POLITICAL REFUGEES

1990 1,536,000

1820 1830 1840 1850 1860 1870 1880 1890 1900 1910 1920 1930 1940 1950 1960 1970 1980 1990

IMMIGRANTS (IN MILLIONS)

NORWAY, SWEDEN AND DENMARK

CANADA AND NEWFOUNDLAND

★ Data not collected 1885–1906

1821 1841 1861 1881 1901 1921

© Copyright HAMMOND INCORPORATED, Maplewood, N.J.
Printed in U.S.A.

Source: *Historical Statistics of the United States*

DISTRIBUTION OF FOREIGN BORN IN UNITED STATES
1910

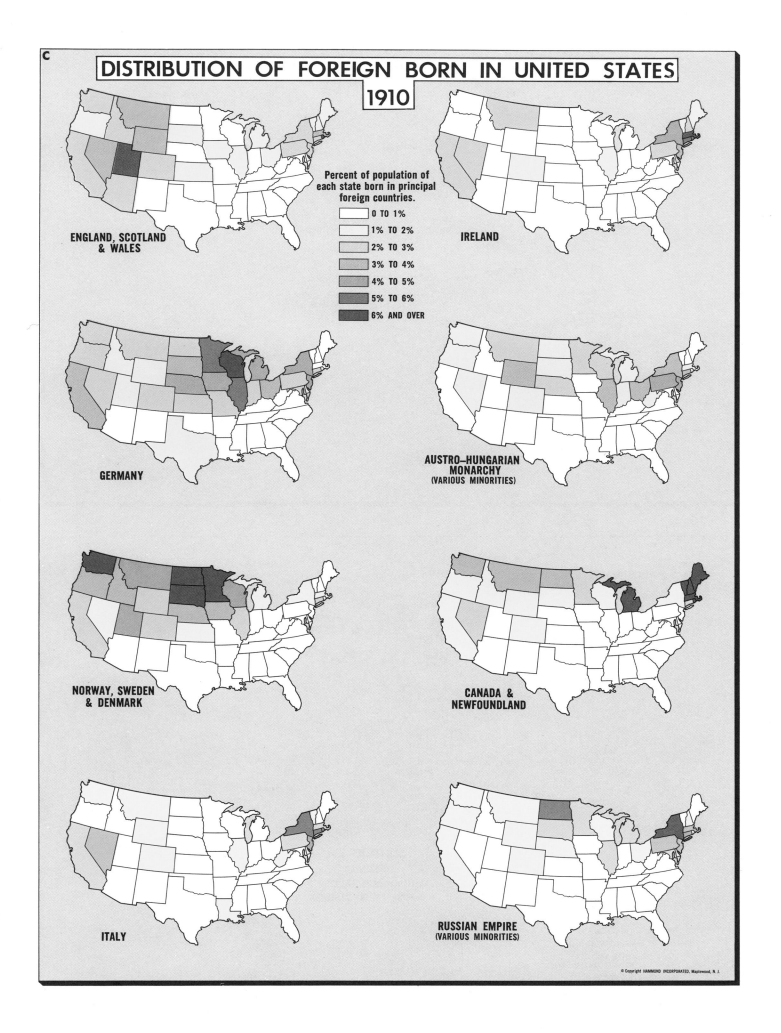

Percent of population of each state born in principal foreign countries.

- 0 TO 1%
- 1% TO 2%
- 2% TO 3%
- 3% TO 4%
- 4% TO 5%
- 5% TO 6%
- 6% AND OVER

ENGLAND, SCOTLAND & WALES

IRELAND

GERMANY

AUSTRO—HUNGARIAN MONARCHY (VARIOUS MINORITIES)

NORWAY, SWEDEN & DENMARK

CANADA & NEWFOUNDLAND

ITALY

RUSSIAN EMPIRE (VARIOUS MINORITIES)

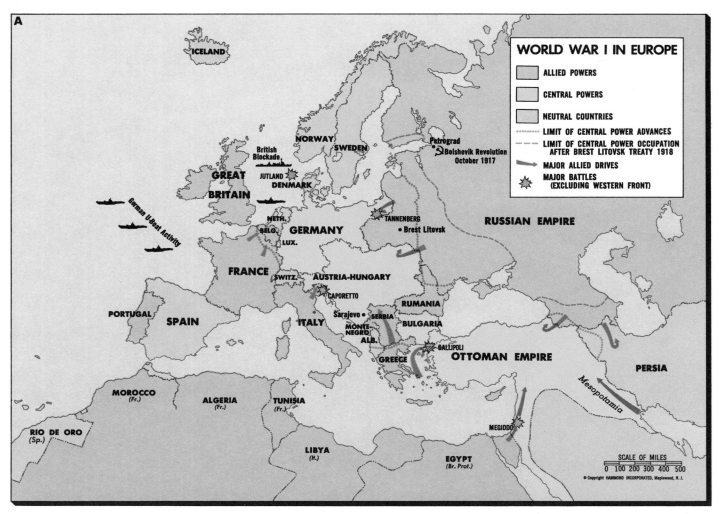

A

WORLD WAR I IN EUROPE

- ALLIED POWERS
- CENTRAL POWERS
- NEUTRAL COUNTRIES
- ········· LIMIT OF CENTRAL POWER ADVANCES
- – – – LIMIT OF CENTRAL POWER OCCUPATION AFTER BREST LITOVSK TREATY 1918
- ➤ MAJOR ALLIED DRIVES
- ✦ MAJOR BATTLES (EXCLUDING WESTERN FRONT)

ICELAND

NORWAY
SWEDEN

GREAT BRITAIN
British Blockade

German U-Boat Activity

JUTLAND
DENMARK

Petrograd
Bolshevik Revolution October 1917

NETH.
BELG.
LUX.
GERMANY

TANNENBERG
• Brest Litovsk

RUSSIAN EMPIRE

FRANCE

SWITZ.
AUSTRIA-HUNGARY

CAPORETTO

ITALY
Sarajevo
SERBIA
MONTE-NEGRO
ALB.
GREECE

RUMANIA
BULGARIA

GALLIPOLI
OTTOMAN EMPIRE

PERSIA

Mesopotamia

PORTUGAL
SPAIN

MOROCCO (Fr.)
ALGERIA (Fr.)
TUNISIA (Fr.)

RIO DE ORO (Sp.)

LIBYA (It.)

EGYPT (Br. Prot.)

MEGIDDO

SCALE OF MILES
0 100 200 300 400 500

© Copyright HAMMOND INCORPORATED, Maplewood, N.J.

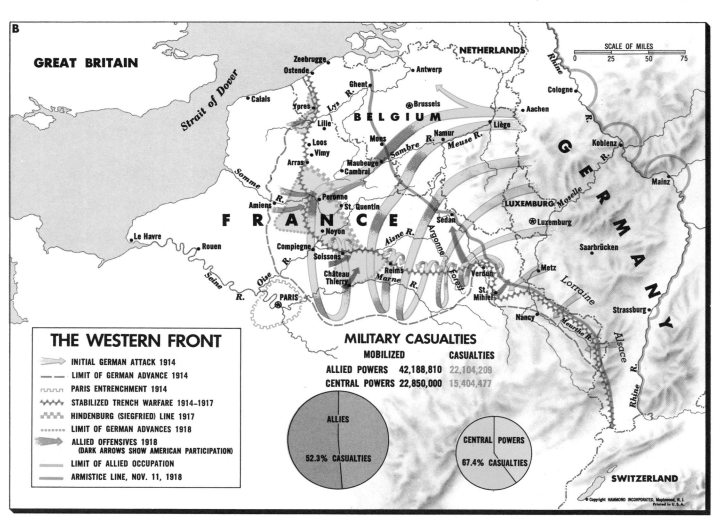

B

GREAT BRITAIN

NETHERLANDS

SCALE OF MILES
0 25 50 75

Strait of Dover

Zeebrugge
Ostende
Calais
Ypres
Lille
Loos
Vimy
Arras

Ghent
Antwerp
BELGIUM
Brussels
Mons
Namur
Maubeuge
Cambrai
Liège
Aachen

Rhine R.
Cologne
Koblenz
Mainz

Somme R.
Peronne
Amiens
St. Quentin
Noyon
Compiegne
Soissons
Château Thierry
Reims
Marne R.

FRANCE

Sambre R.
Meuse R.
Aisne R.
Argonne Forest
Sedan
Verdun
St. Mihiel

LUXEMBURG
Luxemburg
Moselle R.

GERMANY

Le Havre
Rouen
Seine R.
Oise R.

PARIS

Metz
Saarbrücken

Lorraine

Meurthe R.
Nancy
Strassburg

Alsace

Rhine R.

SWITZERLAND

THE WESTERN FRONT

- ➤ INITIAL GERMAN ATTACK 1914
- – – – LIMIT OF GERMAN ADVANCE 1914
- ∿∿∿ PARIS ENTRENCHMENT 1914
- ⋙ STABILIZED TRENCH WARFARE 1914–1917
- ⋘ HINDENBURG (SIEGFRIED) LINE 1917
- ········ LIMIT OF GERMAN ADVANCES 1918
- ➤ ALLIED OFFENSIVES 1918 (DARK ARROWS SHOW AMERICAN PARTICIPATION)
- ─── LIMIT OF ALLIED OCCUPATION
- ─── ARMISTICE LINE, NOV. 11, 1918

MILITARY CASUALTIES

	MOBILIZED	CASUALTIES
ALLIED POWERS	42,188,810	22,104,209
CENTRAL POWERS	22,850,000	15,404,477

ALLIES
52.3% CASUALTIES

CENTRAL POWERS
67.4% CASUALTIES

© Copyright HAMMOND INCORPORATED, Maplewood, N.J.
Printed in U.S.A.

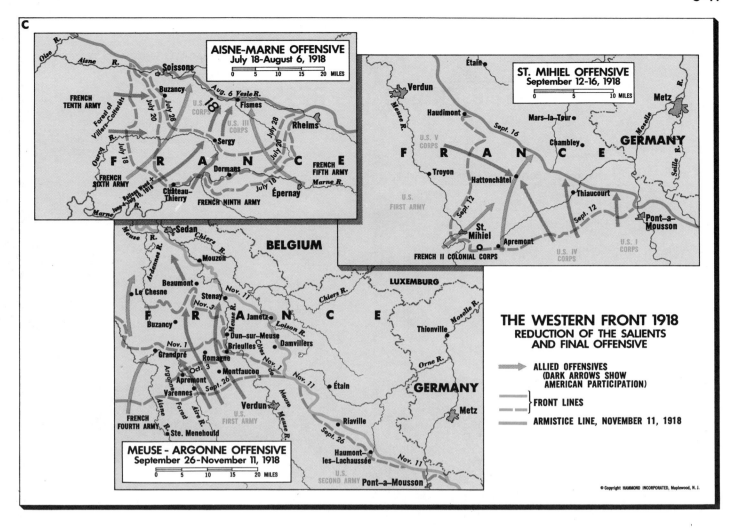

A

THE GREAT DEPRESSION

IN BILLIONS
OF DOLLARS
THE DECLINE AND RECOVERY OF THE NATIONAL ECONOMY

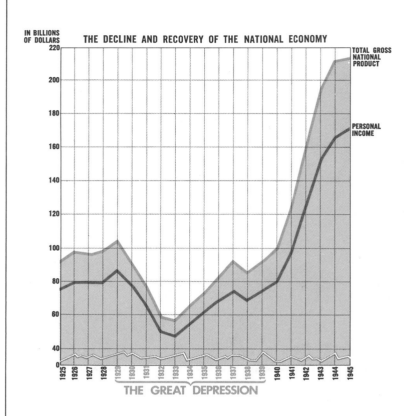

TOTAL GROSS
NATIONAL
PRODUCT

PERSONAL
INCOME

THE GREAT DEPRESSION

NUMBER OF BANK SUSPENSIONS 1919–1933

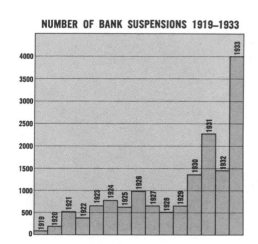

UNEMPLOYMENT
THE UNEMPLOYED AS A PERCENT OF THE CIVILIAN LABOR FORCE

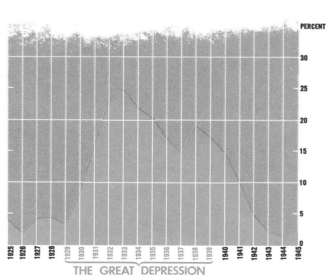

PERCENT

THE GREAT DEPRESSION

HOW U.S. TOTAL PERSONAL INCOME WAS DIVIDED IN 1929

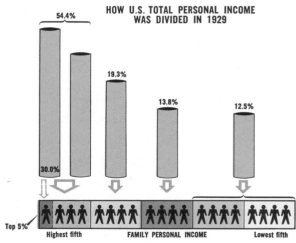

54.4%

30.0%

19.3%

13.8%

12.5%

Top 5%

Highest fifth   FAMILY PERSONAL INCOME   Lowest fifth

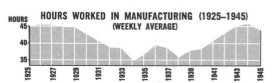

HOURS
HOURS WORKED IN MANUFACTURING (1925–1945)
(WEEKLY AVERAGE)

Source: *Historical Statistics of the United States*

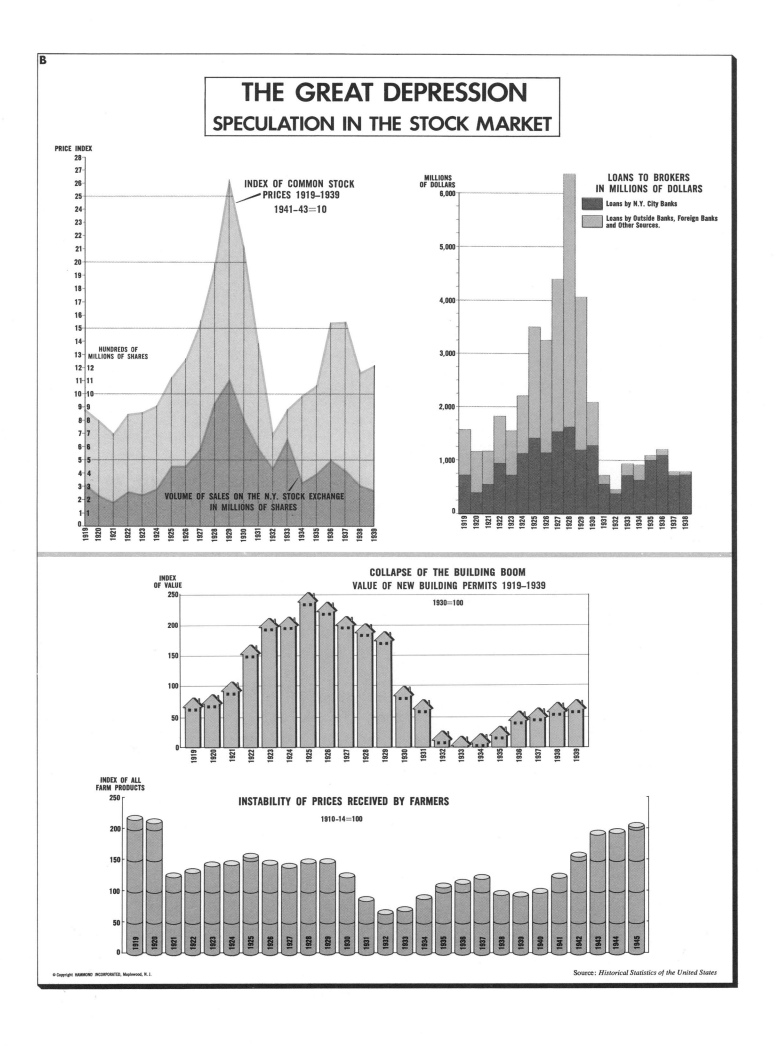

THE GREAT DEPRESSION
SPECULATION IN THE STOCK MARKET

INDEX OF COMMON STOCK PRICES 1919–1939
1941–43=10

PRICE INDEX

HUNDREDS OF MILLIONS OF SHARES

VOLUME OF SALES ON THE N.Y. STOCK EXCHANGE IN MILLIONS OF SHARES

MILLIONS OF DOLLARS

LOANS TO BROKERS IN MILLIONS OF DOLLARS
Loans by N.Y. City Banks
Loans by Outside Banks, Foreign Banks and Other Sources.

INDEX OF VALUE

COLLAPSE OF THE BUILDING BOOM
VALUE OF NEW BUILDING PERMITS 1919–1939
1930=100

INDEX OF ALL FARM PRODUCTS

INSTABILITY OF PRICES RECEIVED BY FARMERS
1910–14=100

© Copyright HAMMOND INCORPORATED, Maplewood, N. J.

Source: *Historical Statistics of the United States*

A

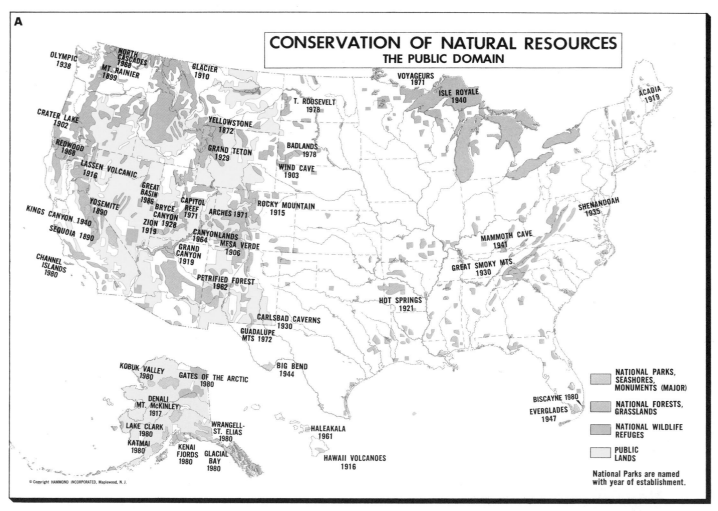

CONSERVATION OF NATURAL RESOURCES
THE PUBLIC DOMAIN

OLYMPIC 1938
NORTH CASCADES 1968
MT. RAINIER 1899
GLACIER 1910
VOYAGEURS 1971
ISLE ROYALE 1940
ACADIA 1919
CRATER LAKE 1902
YELLOWSTONE 1872
T. ROOSEVELT 1978
REDWOOD 1968
GRAND TETON 1929
BADLANDS 1978
LASSEN VOLCANIC 1916
WIND CAVE 1903
SHENANDOAH 1935
GREAT BASIN 1986
YOSEMITE 1890
CAPITOL REEF 1971
ARCHES 1971
ROCKY MOUNTAIN 1915
MAMMOTH CAVE 1941
KINGS CANYON 1940
BRYCE CANYON 1971
ZION 1928
SEQUOIA 1890
CANYONLANDS 1964
MESA VERDE 1906
GREAT SMOKY MTS. 1930
CHANNEL ISLANDS 1980
GRAND CANYON 1919
PETRIFIED FOREST 1962
HOT SPRINGS 1921
CARLSBAD CAVERNS 1930
GUADALUPE MTS 1972
BIG BEND 1944
BISCAYNE 1980
EVERGLADES 1947

KOBUK VALLEY 1980
GATES OF THE ARCTIC 1980
DENALI (MT. McKINLEY) 1917
LAKE CLARK 1980
WRANGELL-ST. ELIAS 1980
KATMAI 1980
KENAI FJORDS 1980
GLACIAL BAY 1980
HALEAKALA 1961
HAWAII VOLCANOES 1916

▨	NATIONAL PARKS, SEASHORES, MONUMENTS (MAJOR)
▨	NATIONAL FORESTS, GRASSLANDS
▨	NATIONAL WILDLIFE REFUGES
▢	PUBLIC LANDS

National Parks are named with year of establishment.

© Copyright HAMMOND INCORPORATED, Maplewood, N.J.

B

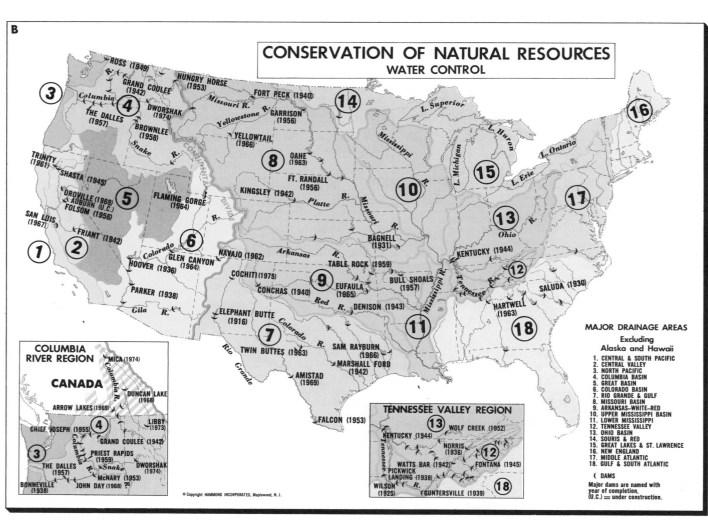

CONSERVATION OF NATURAL RESOURCES
WATER CONTROL

ROSS (1949)
HUNGRY HORSE (1953)
GRAND COULEE (1942)
Columbia R.
FORT PECK (1940)
DWORSHAK (1974)
THE DALLES (1957)
Missouri R.
GARRISON (1956)
Yellowstone R.
BROWNLEE (1958)
Snake R.
YELLOWTAIL (1966)
OAHE (1963)
TRINITY (1961)
SHASTA (1945)
FT. RANDALL (1956)
KINGSLEY (1942)
OROVILLE (1968)
AUBURN (U.C.)
FOLSOM (1956)
FLAMING GORGE (1964)
Platte R.
SAN LUIS (1967)
FRIANT (1942)
Colorado R.
NAVAJO (1962)
Arkansas R.
GLEN CANYON (1964)
BAGNELL (1931)
HOOVER (1936)
COCHITI (1975)
TABLE ROCK (1959)
KENTUCKY (1944)
CONCHAS (1940)
EUFAULA (1965)
BULL SHOALS (1957)
PARKER (1938)
Red R.
DENISON (1943)
Gila R.
ELEPHANT BUTTE (1916)
SALUDA (1930)
HARTWELL (1963)
Colorado R.
SAM RAYBURN (1966)
TWIN BUTTES (1963)
MARSHALL FORD (1942)
Rio Grande
AMISTAD (1969)
FALCON (1953)

L. Superior
L. Huron
L. Michigan
L. Ontario
L. Erie
Mississippi
Ohio
Tennessee
CONTINENTAL DIVIDE

(3) (4) (14) (16) (8) (10) (15) (17) (5) (13) (1) (2) (6) (9) (12) (7) (11) (18)

COLUMBIA RIVER REGION

MICA (1974)
CANADA
Columbia R.
DUNCAN LAKE (1968)
ARROW LAKES (1969)
LIBBY (1973)
CHIEF JOSEPH (1955)
(4)
GRAND COULEE (1942)
PRIEST RAPIDS (1959)
DWORSHAK (1974)
THE DALLES (1957)
Snake R.
McNARY (1953)
(3)
Columbia R.
BONNEVILLE (1938)
JOHN DAY (1968)

© Copyright HAMMOND INCORPORATED, Maplewood, N.J.

TENNESSEE VALLEY REGION

KENTUCKY (1944)
(13)
WOLF CREEK (1952)
NORRIS (1936)
Tennessee R.
WATTS BAR (1942)
(12)
FONTANA (1945)
PICKWICK LANDING (1938)
WILSON (1925)
GUNTERSVILLE (1939)
(18)

MAJOR DRAINAGE AREAS
Excluding Alaska and Hawaii

1. CENTRAL & SOUTH PACIFIC
2. CENTRAL VALLEY
3. NORTH PACIFIC
4. COLUMBIA BASIN
5. GREAT BASIN
6. COLORADO BASIN
7. RIO GRANDE & GULF
8. MISSOURI BASIN
9. ARKANSAS–WHITE–RED
10. UPPER MISSISSIPPI BASIN
11. LOWER MISSISSIPPI
12. TENNESSEE VALLEY
13. OHIO BASIN
14. SOURIS & RED
15. GREAT LAKES & ST. LAWRENCE
16. NEW ENGLAND
17. MIDDLE ATLANTIC
18. GULF & SOUTH ATLANTIC

(DAMS

Major dams are named with year of completion.
(U.C.) = under construction.

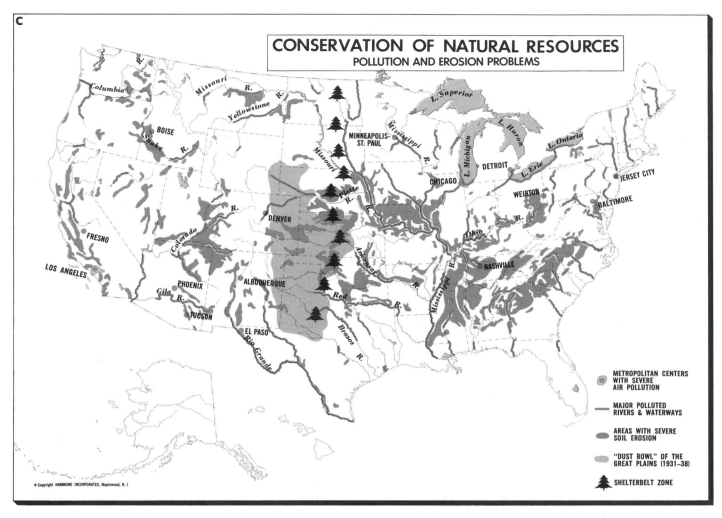

CONSERVATION OF NATURAL RESOURCES
POLLUTION AND EROSION PROBLEMS

METROPOLITAN CENTERS WITH SEVERE AIR POLLUTION

MAJOR POLLUTED RIVERS & WATERWAYS

AREAS WITH SEVERE SOIL EROSION

"DUST BOWL" OF THE GREAT PLAINS (1931–38)

SHELTERBELT ZONE

© Copyright HAMMOND INCORPORATED, Maplewood, N.J.

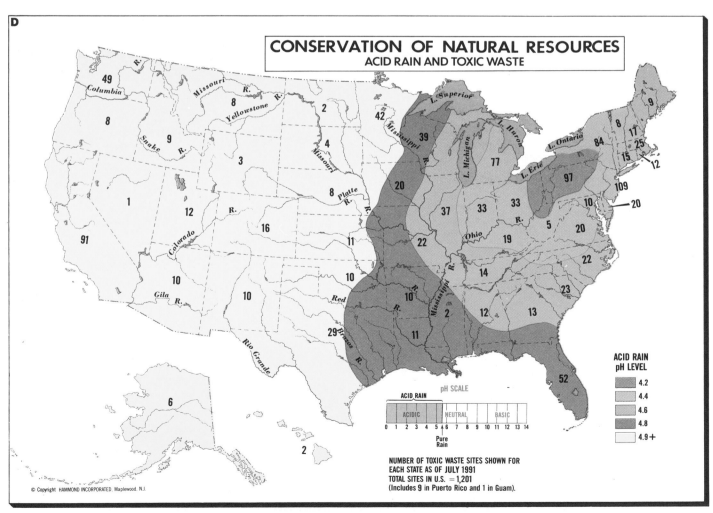

CONSERVATION OF NATURAL RESOURCES
ACID RAIN AND TOXIC WASTE

ACID RAIN pH LEVEL
4.2
4.4
4.6
4.8
4.9+

pH SCALE
ACID RAIN
ACIDIC NEUTRAL BASIC
0 1 2 3 4 5 6 7 8 9 10 11 12 13 14
Pure Rain

NUMBER OF TOXIC WASTE SITES SHOWN FOR
EACH STATE AS OF JULY 1991
TOTAL SITES IN U.S. = 1,201
(Includes 9 in Puerto Rico and 1 in Guam).

© Copyright HAMMOND INCORPORATED, Maplewood, N.J.

A

GERMAN EXPANSION 1935-1939*

SCALE OF MILES

0 100 200 300 400

- Germany 1933
- Area gained by Plebiscite 1935
- Areas annexed 1938
- Area annexed 1939
- German Protectorates

*To Invasion of Poland Sept. 1, 1939

© Copyright HAMMOND INCORPORATED, Maplewood, N.J.

MEMEL To Germany 1939

SAAR To Germany 1935

SUDETENLAND To Germany 1938

Rhineland remilitarized 1936

BOHEMIA & MORAVIA German Protectorate and occupation 1939

AUSTRIA To Germany 1938

SLOVAKIA German Protectorate 1939

Civil War 1936-1939

(To Italy 1939)

B

WORLD WAR II 1939-1940*

SCALE OF MILES

0 100 200 300 400

- Germany and Slovakia
- Allied Nations
- Neutral Nations
- Areas occupied by Germany
- Areas occupied by U.S.S.R.
- German Advances
- British Advances
- Russian Advances

*To July 1, 1940

International Boundaries Sept. 1, 1939

© Copyright HAMMOND INCORPORATED, Maplewood, N.J.

German invasion of Norway and Denmark April 9, 1940

German invasion of Low Countries May 10, 1940

RUSSO-FINNISH WAR 1939-1940

Estonia, Latvia and Lithuania annexed by U.S.S.R. 1940

Battle of France May-June 1940

U.S.S.R. invasion of Poland September 17, 1939

German invasion of Poland September 1, 1939 Start of World War II

Vichy Government established July 1940

Bessarabia and northern Bukovina annexed by U.S.S.R. 1940

Partition of Poland September 27, 1939

Italy declares war on Great Britain and France June 1940

(Italy)

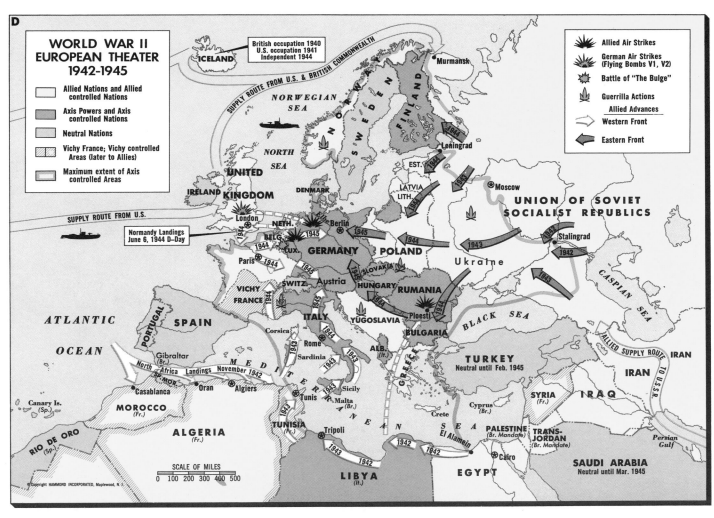

A

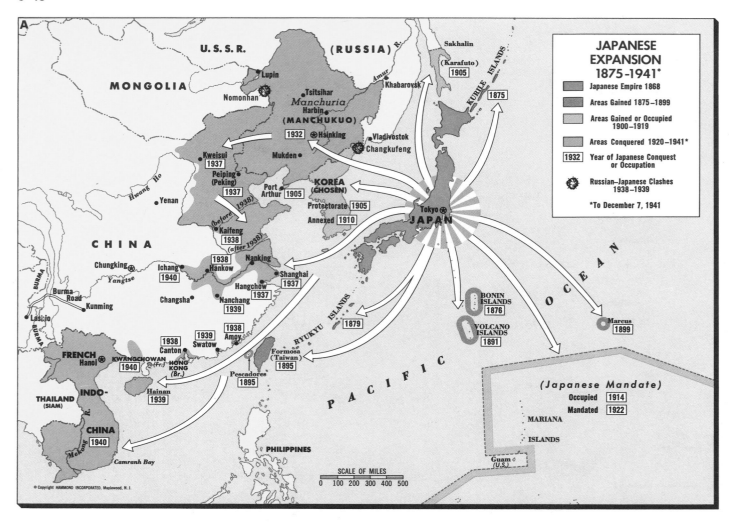

U.S.S.R. (RUSSIA)

MONGOLIA

Sakhalin (Karafuto) 1905

KURILE ISLANDS 1875

Amur R.

Lupin

Nomonhan

Tsitsihar

Manchuria (MANCHUKUO)

Khabarovsk

Harbin

1932 ⊛ Hsinking

Vladivostok

⊛ Changkufeng

Kweisui 1937

Mukden

Peiping (Peking) 1937

Port Arthur 1905

KOREA (CHOSEN)

Yenan

(before 1938)

Protectorate 1905

Annexed 1910

Tokyo ⊛

JAPAN

CHINA

Kaifeng 1938

(after 1938)

1938

Nanking 1937

⊛ Chungking

Ichang 1940

Hankow 1938

Shanghai 1937

RYUKYU ISLANDS 1879

1875

BONIN ISLANDS 1876

VOLCANO ISLANDS 1891

Marcus 1899

Changsha

Hangchow 1937

Nanchang 1939

Yangtse

1938

1939 Swatow

1938

Amoy 1938

Formosa (Taiwan) 1895

BURMA

Burma Road

Kunming

Lashio

BURMA

FRENCH Hanoi ⊛ 1940

KWANGCHOWAN (Fr.)

Canton 1938

HONG KONG (Br.)

Pescadores 1895

PACIFIC

Hainan 1939

THAILAND (SIAM)

INDO-ci.

CHINA 1940

Mekong

Camranh Bay

PHILIPPINES

OCEAN

(Japanese Mandate)

Occupied 1914

Mandated 1922

MARIANA ISLANDS

Guam (U.S.)

JAPANESE EXPANSION 1875–1941*

Japanese Empire 1868

Areas Gained 1875–1899

Areas Gained or Occupied 1900–1919

Areas Conquered 1920–1941*

1932 Year of Japanese Conquest or Occupation

⊛ Russian–Japanese Clashes 1938–1939

*To December 7, 1941

SCALE OF MILES

0 100 200 300 400 500

© Copyright HAMMOND INCORPORATED, Maplewood, N.J.

B

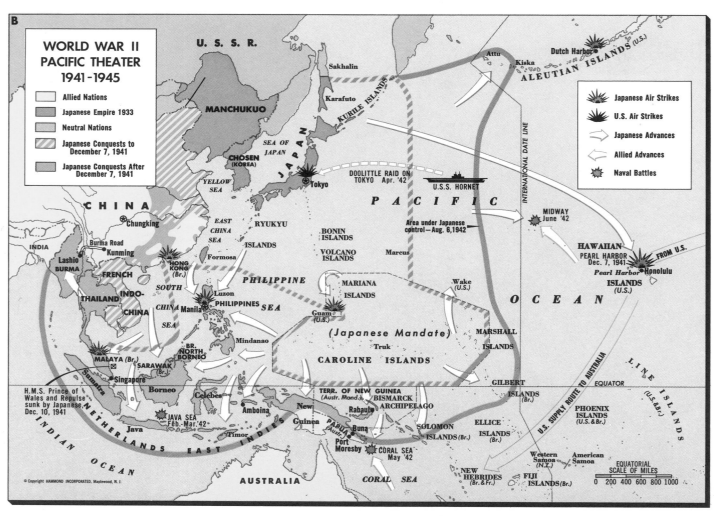

WORLD WAR II PACIFIC THEATER 1941-1945

Allied Nations

Japanese Empire 1933

Neutral Nations

Japanese Conquests to December 7, 1941

Japanese Conquests After December 7, 1941

U.S.S.R.

Sakhalin

Karafuto

MANCHUKUO

KURILE ISLANDS

Attu

Kiska

Dutch Harbor (U.S.)

ALEUTIAN ISLANDS

CHOSEN (KOREA)

SEA OF JAPAN

JAPAN

Tokyo ⊛

DOOLITTLE RAID ON TOKYO Apr. '42

U.S.S. HORNET

INTERNATIONAL DATE LINE

YELLOW SEA

CHINA

⊛ Chungking

EAST CHINA SEA

RYUKYU ISLANDS

Formosa

BONIN ISLANDS

VOLCANO ISLANDS

Marcus

Area under Japanese control—Aug. 6, 1942

MIDWAY June '42

PACIFIC

HAWAIIAN PEARL HARBOR Dec. 7, 1941

FROM U.S.

Pearl Harbor Honolulu

ISLANDS (U.S.)

INDIA

Burma Road

Kunming

Lashio BURMA

FRENCH INDO-CHINA

THAILAND

HONG KONG (Br.)

PHILIPPINE

Luzon

Manila ⊛ PHILIPPINES

SOUTH CHINA SEA

Mindanao

SEA

MARIANA ISLANDS

Guam (U.S.)

Wake (U.S.)

(Japanese Mandate)

Truk

CAROLINE ISLANDS

MARSHALL ISLANDS

OCEAN

LINE ISLANDS (U.S. & Br.)

EQUATOR

H.M.S. Prince of Wales and Repulse sunk by Japanese Dec. 10, 1941

MALAYA (Br.)

SARAWAK (Br.)

Singapore

Sumatra

BR. NORTH BORNEO

Borneo

Celebes

Amboina

NETHERLANDS EAST INDIES

Java

JAVA SEA Feb.-Mar. '42

Timor

TERR. OF NEW GUINEA (Austr. Mand.)

New Guinea

PAPUA (Austr.)

Buna

Port Moresby

CORAL SEA May '42

Rabaul

BISMARCK ARCHIPELAGO

SOLOMON ISLANDS (Br.)

GILBERT ISLANDS (Br.)

ELLICE ISLANDS (Br.)

U.S. SUPPLY ROUTE TO AUSTRALIA

PHOENIX ISLANDS (U.S. & Br.)

INDIAN OCEAN

AUSTRALIA

CORAL SEA

NEW HEBRIDES (Br. & Fr.)

FIJI ISLANDS (Br.)

Western Samoa (N.Z.)

American Samoa

EQUATORIAL SCALE OF MILES

0 200 400 600 800 1000

© Copyright HAMMOND INCORPORATED, Maplewood, N.J.

Japanese Air Strikes

U.S. Air Strikes

Japanese Advances

Allied Advances

Naval Battles

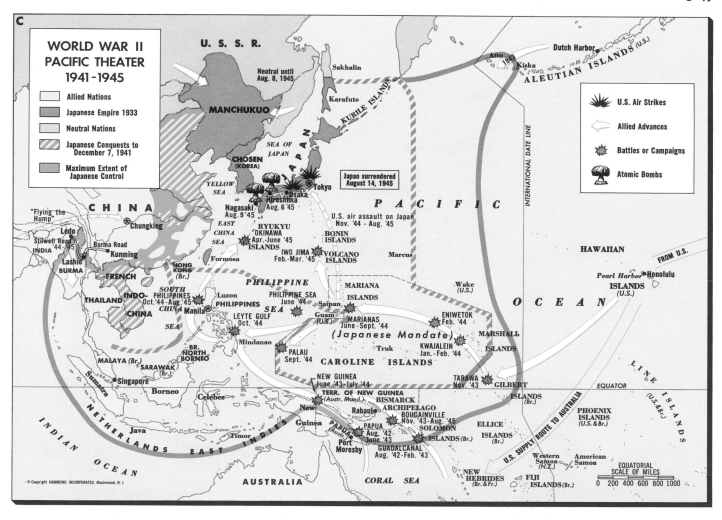

C

WORLD WAR II PACIFIC THEATER 1941-1945

Allied Nations
Japanese Empire 1933
Neutral Nations
Japanese Conquests to December 7, 1941
Maximum Extent of Japanese Control

U.S. Air Strikes
Allied Advances
Battles or Campaigns
Atomic Bombs

U. S. S. R.

Neutral until Aug. 8, 1945

Sakhalin

Karafuto

MANCHUKUO

KURILE ISLANDS

SEA OF JAPAN

CHOSEN (KOREA)

JAPAN

Attu 1943

Kiska

Dutch Harbor

ALEUTIAN ISLANDS (U.S.)

INTERNATIONAL DATE LINE

Japan surrendered August 14, 1945

PACIFIC

YELLOW SEA

Nagasaki Aug. 9 '45

Hiroshima Aug. 6 '45

Osaka

Tokyo

EAST CHINA SEA

C H I N A

"Flying the Hump"

Ledo

Stilwell Road '44 '45

INDIA

Chungking

Burma Road

Kunming

Lashio

BURMA

FRENCH

INDO-

THAILAND

CHINA

RYUKYU OKINAWA Apr.-June '45 ISLANDS

Formosa

U.S. air assault on Japan Nov. '44 - Aug. '45

IWO JIMA Feb.-Mar. '45

VOLCANO ISLANDS

BONIN ISLANDS

Marcus

HAWAIIAN

HONG KONG (Br.)

SOUTH PHILIPPINES Oct.'44-Aug.'45

PHILIPPINES

Luzon

PHILIPPINE SEA June '44

Manila

MARIANA ISLANDS

Saipan

Wake (U.S.)

Pearl Harbor

Honolulu

ISLANDS (U.S.)

O C E A N

LEYTE GULF Oct. '44

Guam (U.S.)

MARIANAS June-Sept. '44

(Japanese Mandate)

ENIWETOK Feb. '44

MARSHALL

Mindanao

Truk

KWAJALEIN Jan.- Feb. '44

ISLANDS

MALAYA (Br.)

BR. NORTH BORNEO

SARAWAK (Br.)

PALAU Sept. '44

CAROLINE ISLANDS

Singapore

Borneo

Celebes

Sumatra

NETHERLANDS EAST INDIES

Java

Timor

NEW GUINEA June '43-July '44

TERR. OF NEW GUINEA (Austr. Mand.)

BISMARCK ARCHIPELAGO

New Guinea

Rabaul

BOUGAINVILLE Nov. '43-Aug. '45

PAPUA (Austr.)

Port Moresby

PAPUA Aug. '42-June '43

SOLOMON ISLANDS (Br.)

GUADALCANAL Aug. '42-Feb. '43

TARAWA Nov. '43

GILBERT ISLANDS (Br.)

EQUATOR

LINE ISLANDS (U.S.&Br.)

ELLICE ISLANDS (Br.)

PHOENIX ISLANDS (U.S.& Br.)

U.S. SUPPLY ROUTE TO AUSTRALIA

FROM U.S.

Western Samoa (N.Z.)

American Samoa

NEW HEBRIDES (Br. & Fr.)

FIJI ISLANDS (Br.)

EQUATORIAL SCALE OF MILES
0 200 400 600 800 1000

INDIAN OCEAN

AUSTRALIA

CORAL SEA

© Copyright HAMMOND INCORPORATED, Maplewood, N. J.

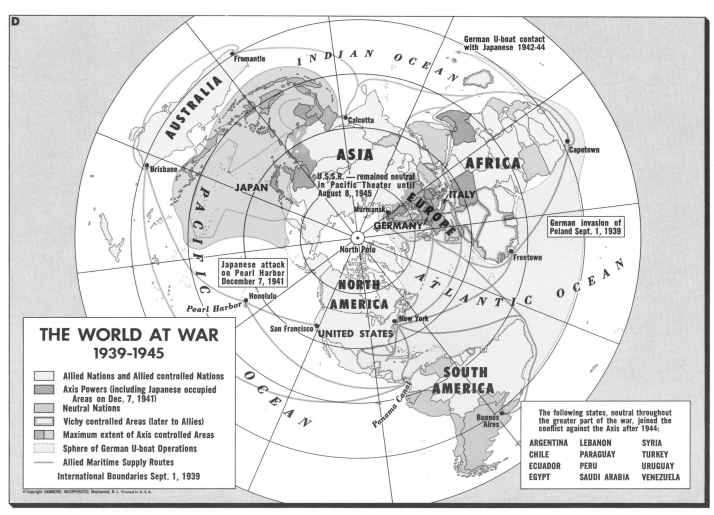

D

German U-boat contact with Japanese 1942-44

Fremantle

INDIAN OCEAN

AUSTRALIA

Calcutta

Capetown

ASIA

AFRICA

Brisbane

PACIFIC

JAPAN

U.S.S.R. — remained neutral in Pacific Theater until August 8, 1945

ITALY

EUROPE

Murmansk

GERMANY

German invasion of Poland Sept. 1, 1939

North Pole

Freetown

Japanese attack on Pearl Harbor December 7, 1941

NORTH AMERICA

ATLANTIC OCEAN

Honolulu

Pearl Harbor

San Francisco

UNITED STATES

New York

THE WORLD AT WAR 1939-1945

Allied Nations and Allied controlled Nations
Axis Powers (including Japanese occupied Areas on Dec. 7, 1941)
Neutral Nations
Vichy controlled Areas (later to Allies)
Maximum extent of Axis controlled Areas
Sphere of German U-boat Operations
Allied Maritime Supply Routes
International Boundaries Sept. 1, 1939

SOUTH AMERICA

Panama Canal

OCEAN

Buenos Aires

The following states, neutral throughout the greater part of the war, joined the conflict against the Axis after 1944:

ARGENTINA LEBANON SYRIA
CHILE PARAGUAY TURKEY
ECUADOR PERU URUGUAY
EGYPT SAUDI ARABIA VENEZUELA

© Copyright HAMMOND INCORPORATED, Maplewood, N.J. Printed in U.S.A.

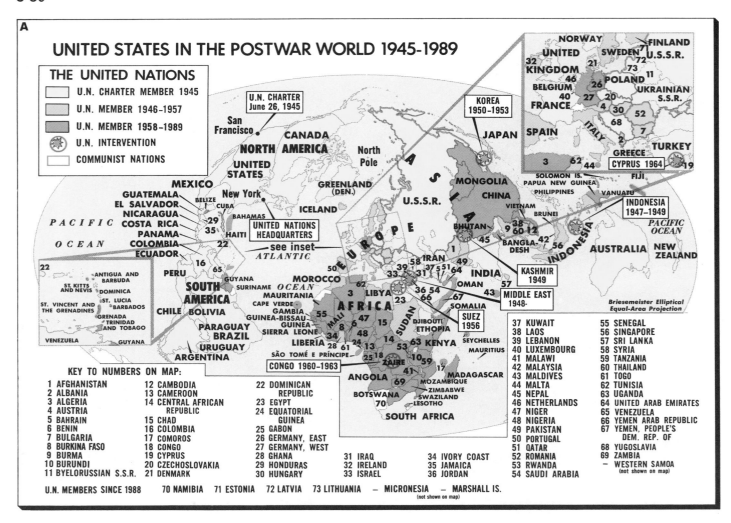

A

UNITED STATES IN THE POSTWAR WORLD 1945-1989

THE UNITED NATIONS

- U.N. CHARTER MEMBER 1945
- U.N. MEMBER 1946–1957
- U.N. MEMBER 1958–1989
- U.N. INTERVENTION
- COMMUNIST NATIONS

U.N. CHARTER June 26, 1945

KOREA 1950–1953

San Francisco

CANADA

NORTH AMERICA

North Pole

JAPAN

UNITED STATES

GREENLAND (DEN.)

MONGOLIA

CHINA

MEXICO

GUATEMALA
EL SALVADOR
NICARAGUA
COSTA RICA
PANAMA
COLOMBIA
ECUADOR

BELIZE
CUBA
BAHAMAS
HAITI

NEW YORK

ICELAND

U.S.S.R.

VIETNAM

PHILIPPINES

BRUNEI

INDONESIA 1947–1949

UNITED NATIONS HEADQUARTERS
see inset

PACIFIC OCEAN

ATLANTIC

PERU

SOUTH AMERICA

CHILE BOLIVIA

PARAGUAY
BRAZIL
URUGUAY
ARGENTINA

GUYANA
SURINAME
MAURITANIA
CAPE VERDE
GAMBIA
GUINEA-BISSAU
GUINEA
SIERRA LEONE
LIBERIA

MOROCCO

ALGERIA
LIBYA

AFRICA

MALI

SUDAN

IRAN

INDIA

KASHMIR 1949

OMAN

SOMALIA

MIDDLE EAST 1948-

ETHIOPIA

DJIBOUTI

KENYA

SEYCHELLES
MAURITIUS

SUEZ 1956

CONGO 1960–1963

SÃO TOMÉ E PRÍNCIPE

ZAIRE

ANGOLA

ZAMBIA

BOTSWANA

MOZAMBIQUE
ZIMBABWE
SWAZILAND
LESOTHO

MADAGASCAR

SOUTH AFRICA

AUSTRALIA NEW ZEALAND

PACIFIC OCEAN

SOLOMON IS.
PAPUA NEW GUINEA
VANUATU
FIJI

Briesemeister Elliptical Equal-Area Projection

ANTIGUA AND BARBUDA
ST. KITTS AND NEVIS
DOMINICA
ST. LUCIA BARBADOS
ST. VINCENT AND THE GRENADINES
GRENADA
TRINIDAD AND TOBAGO
VENEZUELA
GUYANA

NORWAY · FINLAND · SWEDEN · U.S.S.R.

UNITED KINGDOM · POLAND · UKRAINIAN S.S.R.
BELGIUM · FRANCE · ITALY · SPAIN · GREECE · TURKEY
CYPRUS 1964

KEY TO NUMBERS ON MAP:

1 AFGHANISTAN	12 CAMBODIA	22 DOMINICAN REPUBLIC	37 KUWAIT
2 ALBANIA	13 CAMEROON	23 EGYPT	38 LAOS
3 ALGERIA	14 CENTRAL AFRICAN REPUBLIC	24 EQUATORIAL GUINEA	39 LEBANON
4 AUSTRIA	15 CHAD	25 GABON	40 LUXEMBOURG
5 BAHRAIN	16 COLOMBIA	26 GERMANY, EAST	41 MALAWI
6 BENIN	17 COMOROS	27 GERMANY, WEST	42 MALAYSIA
7 BULGARIA	18 CONGO	28 GHANA	43 MALDIVES
8 BURKINA FASO	19 CYPRUS	29 HONDURAS	44 MALTA
9 BURMA	20 CZECHOSLOVAKIA	30 HUNGARY	45 NEPAL
10 BURUNDI	21 DENMARK	31 IRAQ	46 NETHERLANDS
11 BYELORUSSIAN S.S.R.		32 IRELAND	47 NIGER
		33 ISRAEL	48 NIGERIA
		34 IVORY COAST	49 PAKISTAN
		35 JAMAICA	50 PORTUGAL
		36 JORDAN	51 QATAR

52 ROMANIA	55 SENEGAL
53 RWANDA	56 SINGAPORE
54 SAUDI ARABIA	57 SRI LANKA
	58 SYRIA
	59 TANZANIA
	60 THAILAND
	61 TOGO
	62 TUNISIA
	63 UGANDA
	64 UNITED ARAB EMIRATES
	65 VENEZUELA
	66 YEMEN ARAB REPUBLIC
	67 YEMEN, PEOPLE'S DEM. REP. OF
	68 YUGOSLAVIA
	69 ZAMBIA
	– WESTERN SAMOA (not shown on map)

U.N. MEMBERS SINCE 1988   70 NAMIBIA   71 ESTONIA   72 LATVIA   73 LITHUANIA   – MICRONESIA   – MARSHALL IS. (not shown on map)

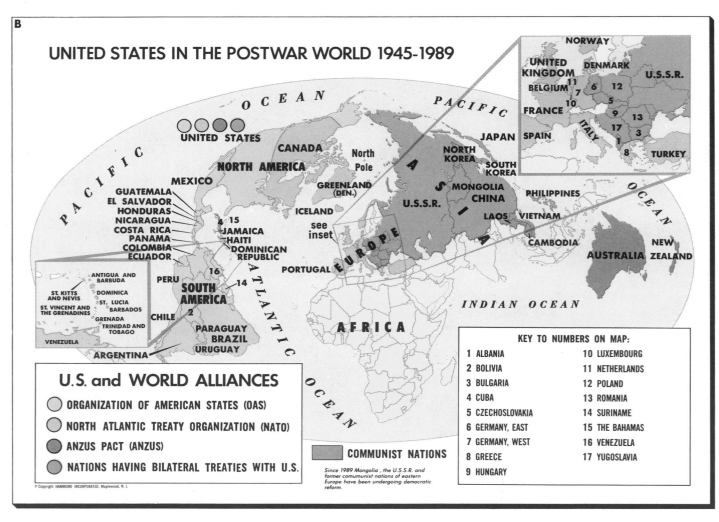

B

UNITED STATES IN THE POSTWAR WORLD 1945-1989

OCEAN

PACIFIC

UNITED STATES

CANADA

NORTH AMERICA

North Pole

JAPAN

NORTH KOREA

SOUTH KOREA

MONGOLIA

CHINA

MEXICO

GREENLAND (DEN.)

ICELAND

U.S.S.R.

GUATEMALA
EL SALVADOR
HONDURAS
NICARAGUA
COSTA RICA
PANAMA
COLOMBIA
ECUADOR

JAMAICA
HAITI
DOMINICAN REPUBLIC

see inset

EUROPE

ASIA

PHILIPPINES

LAOS

VIETNAM

CAMBODIA

NEW ZEALAND

AUSTRALIA

PERU

SOUTH AMERICA

PORTUGAL

ATLANTIC

INDIAN OCEAN

AFRICA

CHILE

PARAGUAY
BRAZIL
URUGUAY
ARGENTINA

OCEAN

ANTIGUA AND BARBUDA
ST. KITTS AND NEVIS
DOMINICA
ST. LUCIA BARBADOS
ST. VINCENT AND THE GRENADINES
GRENADA
TRINIDAD AND TOBAGO
VENEZUELA

NORWAY

UNITED KINGDOM · DENMARK · U.S.S.R.
BELGIUM · FRANCE · ITALY · SPAIN · TURKEY

U.S. and WORLD ALLIANCES

- ORGANIZATION OF AMERICAN STATES (OAS)
- NORTH ATLANTIC TREATY ORGANIZATION (NATO)
- ANZUS PACT (ANZUS)
- NATIONS HAVING BILATERAL TREATIES WITH U.S.

COMMUNIST NATIONS

Since 1989 Mongolia, the U.S.S.R. and former communist nations of eastern Europe have been undergoing democratic reform.

KEY TO NUMBERS ON MAP:

1 ALBANIA	10 LUXEMBOURG
2 BOLIVIA	11 NETHERLANDS
3 BULGARIA	12 POLAND
4 CUBA	13 ROMANIA
5 CZECHOSLOVAKIA	14 SURINAME
6 GERMANY, EAST	15 THE BAHAMAS
7 GERMANY, WEST	16 VENEZUELA
8 GREECE	17 YUGOSLAVIA
9 HUNGARY	

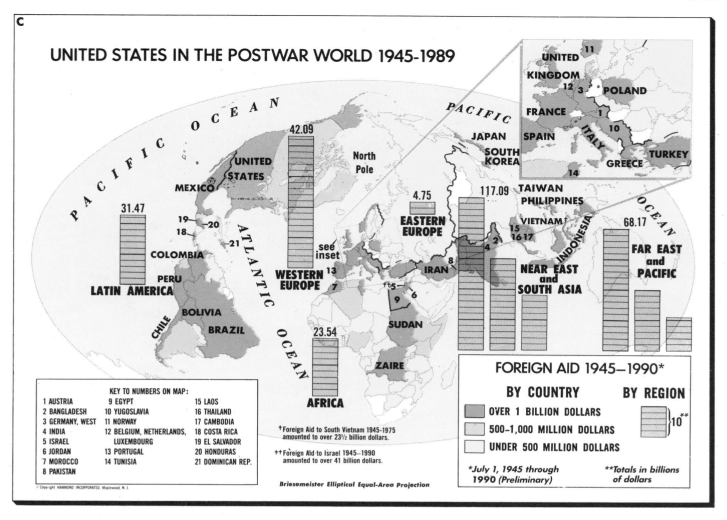

UNITED STATES IN THE POSTWAR WORLD 1945-1989

KEY TO NUMBERS ON MAP:

1 AUSTRIA	9 EGYPT	15 LAOS
2 BANGLADESH	10 YUGOSLAVIA	16 THAILAND
3 GERMANY, WEST	11 NORWAY	17 CAMBODIA
4 INDIA	12 BELGIUM, NETHERLANDS,	18 COSTA RICA
5 ISRAEL	LUXEMBOURG	19 EL SALVADOR
6 JORDAN	13 PORTUGAL	20 HONDURAS
7 MOROCCO	14 TUNISIA	21 DOMINICAN REP.
8 PAKISTAN		

†Foreign Aid to South Vietnam 1945-1975 amounted to over 23½ billion dollars.

††Foreign Aid to Israel 1945-1990 amounted to over 41 billion dollars.

Briesemeister Elliptical Equal-Area Projection

FOREIGN AID 1945–1990*

BY COUNTRY
- OVER 1 BILLION DOLLARS
- 500–1,000 MILLION DOLLARS
- UNDER 500 MILLION DOLLARS

BY REGION }10**

*July 1, 1945 through 1990 (Preliminary)
**Totals in billions of dollars

© Copyright HAMMOND INCORPORATED, Maplewood, N. J.

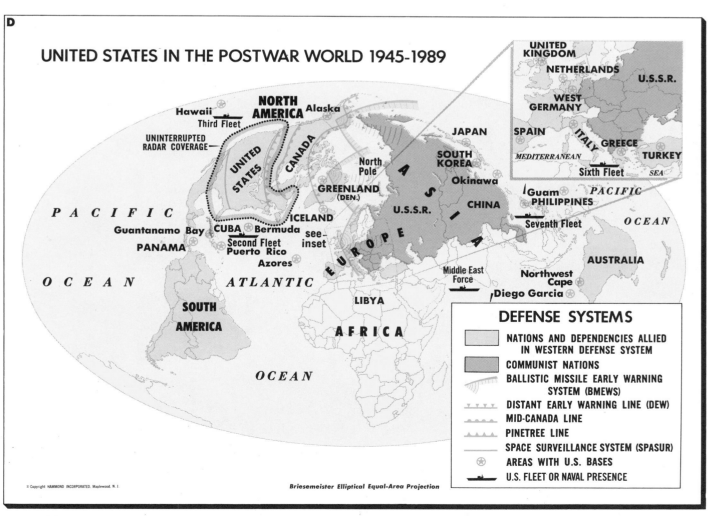

UNITED STATES IN THE POSTWAR WORLD 1945-1989

DEFENSE SYSTEMS
- NATIONS AND DEPENDENCIES ALLIED IN WESTERN DEFENSE SYSTEM
- COMMUNIST NATIONS
- BALLISTIC MISSILE EARLY WARNING SYSTEM (BMEWS)
- DISTANT EARLY WARNING LINE (DEW)
- MID-CANADA LINE
- PINETREE LINE
- SPACE SURVEILLANCE SYSTEM (SPASUR)
- AREAS WITH U.S. BASES
- U.S. FLEET OR NAVAL PRESENCE

© Copyright HAMMOND INCORPORATED, Maplewood, N. J.

Briesemeister Elliptical Equal-Area Projection

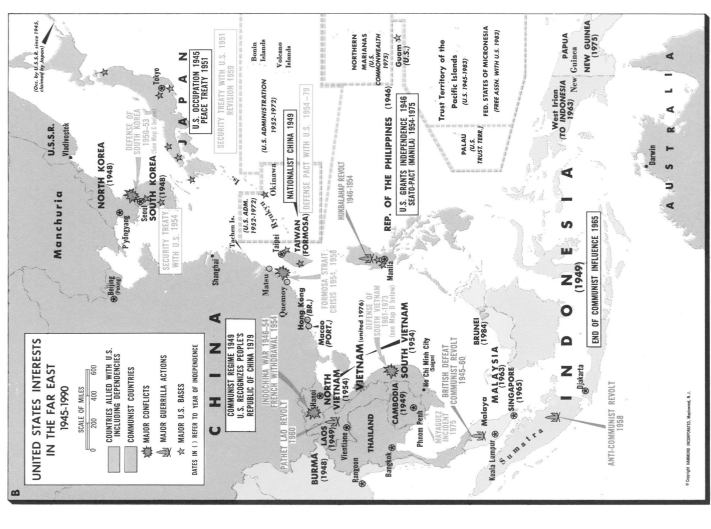

B. UNITED STATES INTERESTS IN THE FAR EAST 1945-1990

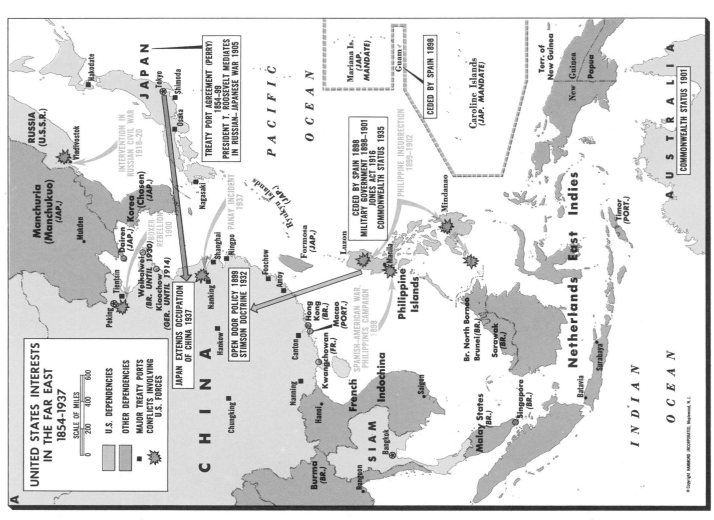

A. UNITED STATES INTERESTS IN THE FAR EAST 1854-1937

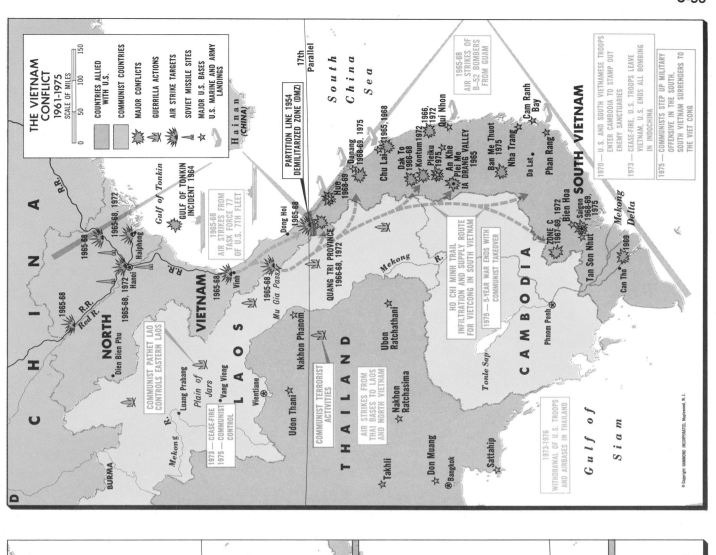

THE VIETNAM CONFLICT 1961-1975

SCALE OF MILES

COUNTRIES ALLIED WITH U.S.

COMMUNIST COUNTRIES

MAJOR CONFLICTS

GUERRILLA ACTIONS

AIR STRIKE TARGETS

SOVIET MISSILE SITES

U.S. MARINE AND ARMY LANDINGS

1965-68 AIR STRIKES FROM TASK FORCE 77 OF U.S. 7TH FLEET

1965-68 AIR STRIKES OF B-52 BOMBERS FROM GUAM

GULF OF TONKIN INCIDENT 1964

PARTITION LINE 1954 DEMILITARIZED ZONE (DMZ)

17th Parallel

1970 — U.S. AND SOUTH VIETNAMESE TROOPS ENTER CAMBODIA TO STAMP OUT ENEMY SANCTUARIES

1973 — CEASE-FIRE, U.S. TROOPS LEAVE VIETNAM, U.S. ENDS ALL BOMBING IN INDOCHINA

1975 — COMMUNISTS STEP UP MILITARY OFFENSIVE IN THE SOUTH, SOUTH VIETNAM SURRENDERS TO THE VIET CONG

South China Sea

Hainan (CHINA)

Gulf of Tonkin

CHINA

NORTH VIETNAM

Red R.

R.R.

R.R.

Dien Bien Phu

Hanoi

Haiphong

1965-68

1965-68, 1972

1965-68

Dong Hoi

Vinh

Mu Gia Pass

1965-68

1965-68

1965-68

Hue 1968-69

QUANG TRI PROVINCE 1966-68, 1972

Danang 1968-69, 1975

Chu Lai 1965, 1968

Dak To 1966-68

Kontum 1972, 1966, 1972

Pleiku 1975

An Khe 1975

Qui Nhon

Ban Me Thuot 1975

Nha Trang

Da Lat.

Cam Ranh Bay

Phan Rang

SOUTH VIETNAM

IA DRANG VALLEY 1965

Plei Me

ZONE C 1967-69, 1972

Bien Hoa 1975

Saigon 1968-69, 1975

Tan Son Nhut 1975

Can Tho 1969

Phnom Penh

CAMBODIA

Mekong R.

Tonle Sap

Mekong Delta

COMMUNIST PATHET LAO CONTROLS EASTERN LAOS

Luang Prabang

Plain of Jars

Vang Vieng

Vientiane

Mekong R.

BURMA

LAOS

1973 — CEASE-FIRE 1975 — COMMUNIST CONTROL

Nakhon Phanom

Udon Thani

Nakhon Ratchasima

Ubon Ratchathani

COMMUNIST TERRORIST ACTIVITIES

AIR STRIKES FROM THAI BASES TO LAOS AND NORTH VIETNAM

HO CHI MINH TRAIL INFILTRATION AND SUPPLY ROUTE FOR VIETCONG IN SOUTH VIETNAM

1975 — 5-YEAR WAR ENDS WITH COMMUNIST TAKEOVER

THAILAND

Takhli

Don Muang

Bangkok

Sattahip

Gulf of Siam

1973-1976 WITHDRAWAL OF U.S. TROOPS AND AIRBASES IN THAILAND

© Copyright HAMMOND INCORPORATED, Maplewood, N.J.

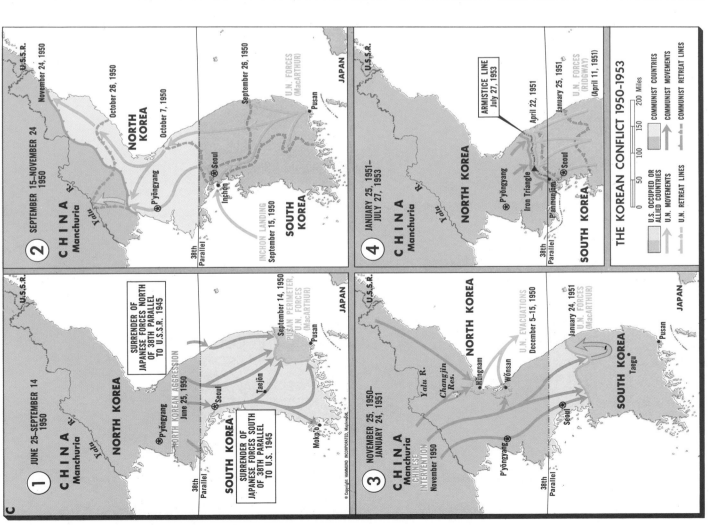

THE KOREAN CONFLICT 1950-1953

① JUNE 25—SEPTEMBER 14 1950

U.S.S.R.

CHINA

Manchuria

NORTH KOREA

Yalu

Pyongyang

Seoul

NORTH KOREAN AGGRESSION June 25, 1950

Taejon

SURRENDER OF JAPANESE FORCES NORTH OF 38TH PARALLEL TO U.S.S.R. 1945

SURRENDER OF JAPANESE FORCES SOUTH OF 38TH PARALLEL TO U.S. 1945

38th Parallel

SOUTH KOREA

Mokp'o

PUSAN PERIMETER, U.N. FORCES (MacARTHUR)

September 14, 1950

Pusan

JAPAN

② SEPTEMBER 15—NOVEMBER 24 1950

U.S.S.R.

November 24, 1950

October 26, 1950

October 7, 1950

CHINA

Manchuria

Yalu

NORTH KOREA

Pyongyang

September 26, 1950

U.N. FORCES (MacARTHUR)

Seoul

Inchon

38th Parallel

SOUTH KOREA

INCHON LANDING September 15, 1950

Pusan

JAPAN

③ NOVEMBER 25, 1950— JANUARY 24, 1951

U.S.S.R.

CHINA

Manchuria

CHINESE INTERVENTION November 1950

Yalu R.

Changjin Res.

NORTH KOREA

Hungnam

Wonsan

U.N. EVACUATIONS December 5-15, 1950

January 24, 1951 U.N. FORCES (MacARTHUR)

Pyongyang

Seoul

38th Parallel

SOUTH KOREA

Taegu

Pusan

JAPAN

④ JANUARY 25, 1951— JULY 27, 1953

U.S.S.R.

CHINA

Manchuria

NORTH KOREA

Pyongyang

ARMISTICE LINE July 27, 1953

April 22, 1951

January 25, 1951, U.N. FORCES (RIDGWAY) (April 11, 1951)

Iron Triangle

P'anmunjom

Seoul

38th Parallel

SOUTH KOREA

200 Miles

COMMUNIST COUNTRIES

COMMUNIST MOVEMENTS

COMMUNIST RETREAT LINES

U.S. OCCUPIED OR ALLIED COUNTRIES

U.N. MOVEMENTS

U.N. RETREAT LINES

© Copyright HAMMOND INCORPORATED, Maplewood, N.J.

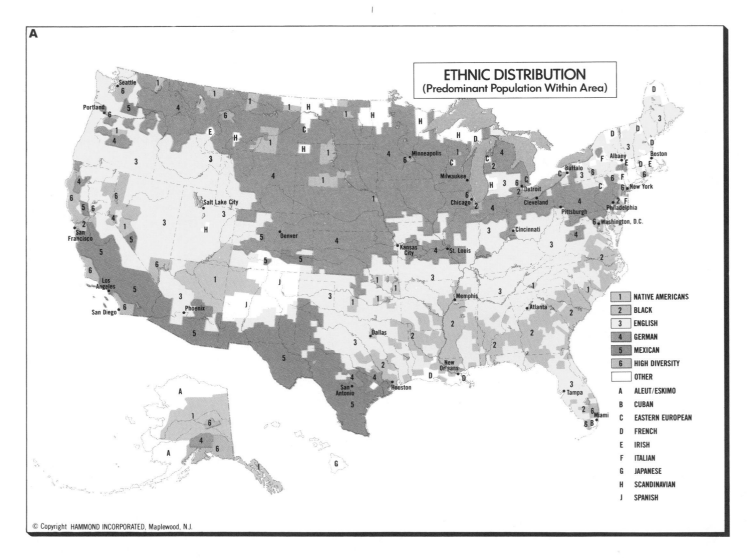

ETHNIC DISTRIBUTION
(Predominant Population Within Area)

1	NATIVE AMERICANS
2	BLACK
3	ENGLISH
4	GERMAN
5	MEXICAN
6	HIGH DIVERSITY
	OTHER
A	ALEUT/ESKIMO
B	CUBAN
C	EASTERN EUROPEAN
D	FRENCH
E	IRISH
F	ITALIAN
G	JAPANESE
H	SCANDINAVIAN
J	SPANISH

© Copyright HAMMOND INCORPORATED, Maplewood, N.J.

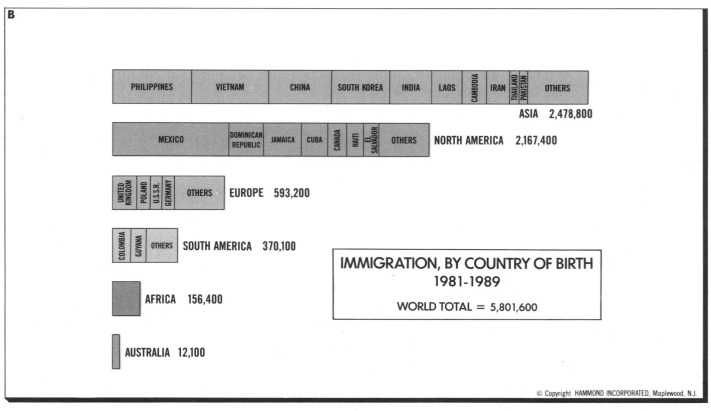

IMMIGRATION, BY COUNTRY OF BIRTH
1981-1989

WORLD TOTAL = 5,801,600

ASIA 2,478,800
NORTH AMERICA 2,167,400
EUROPE 593,200
SOUTH AMERICA 370,100
AFRICA 156,400
AUSTRALIA 12,100

© Copyright HAMMOND INCORPORATED, Maplewood, N.J.

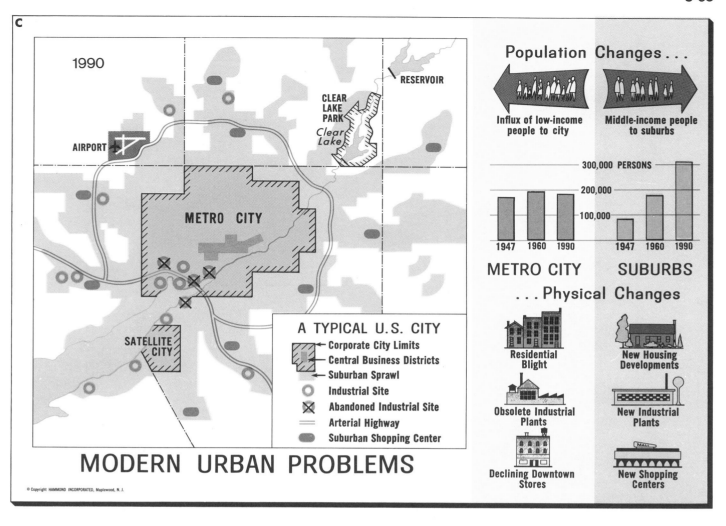

C

1990

RESERVOIR

CLEAR LAKE PARK
Clear Lake

AIRPORT

METRO CITY

SATELLITE CITY

A TYPICAL U.S. CITY
- ⬚ ← Corporate City Limits
- ← Central Business Districts
- ← Suburban Sprawl
- ○ Industrial Site
- ✕ Abandoned Industrial Site
- ═ Arterial Highway
- ⬤ Suburban Shopping Center

MODERN URBAN PROBLEMS

© Copyright HAMMOND INCORPORATED, Maplewood, N. J.

Population Changes...

Influx of low-income people to city ← → **Middle-income people to suburbs**

300,000 PERSONS
200,000
100,000

1947	1960	1990	1947	1960	1990

METRO CITY   **SUBURBS**

...Physical Changes

Residential Blight — New Housing Developments

Obsolete Industrial Plants — New Industrial Plants

Declining Downtown Stores — New Shopping Centers

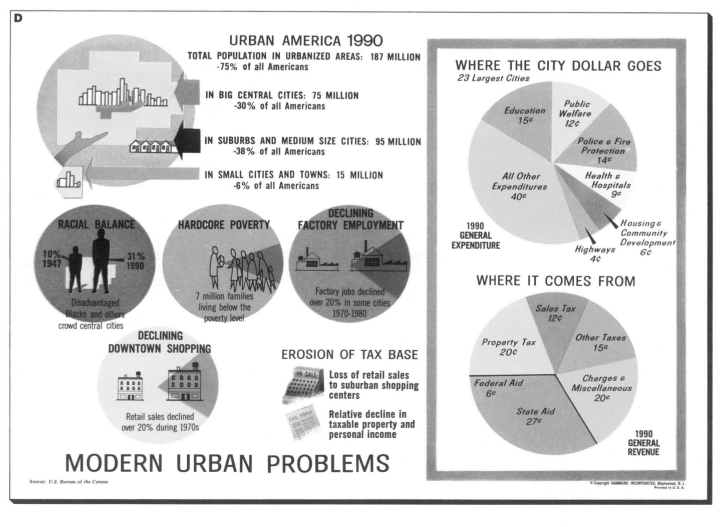

D

URBAN AMERICA 1990

TOTAL POPULATION IN URBANIZED AREAS: 187 MILLION
-75% of all Americans

IN BIG CENTRAL CITIES: 75 MILLION
-30% of all Americans

IN SUBURBS AND MEDIUM SIZE CITIES: 95 MILLION
-38% of all Americans

IN SMALL CITIES AND TOWNS: 15 MILLION
-6% of all Americans

RACIAL BALANCE
10% 1947 — 31% 1990
Disadvantaged Blacks and others crowd central cities

HARDCORE POVERTY
7 million families living below the poverty level

DECLINING FACTORY EMPLOYMENT
Factory jobs declined over 20% in some cities 1970-1980

DECLINING DOWNTOWN SHOPPING
Retail sales declined over 20% during 1970s

EROSION OF TAX BASE
Loss of retail sales to suburban shopping centers

Relative decline in taxable property and personal income

WHERE THE CITY DOLLAR GOES
23 Largest Cities

- Education 15¢
- Public Welfare 12¢
- Police & Fire Protection 14¢
- Health & Hospitals 9¢
- Housing & Community Development 6¢
- Highways 4¢
- All Other Expenditures 40¢

1990 GENERAL EXPENDITURE

WHERE IT COMES FROM

- Sales Tax 12¢
- Other Taxes 15¢
- Property Tax 20¢
- Charges & Miscellaneous 20¢
- Federal Aid 6¢
- State Aid 27¢

1990 GENERAL REVENUE

MODERN URBAN PROBLEMS

Source: *U.S. Bureau of the Census*

© Copyright HAMMOND INCORPORATED, Maplewood, N. J. Printed in U. S. A.

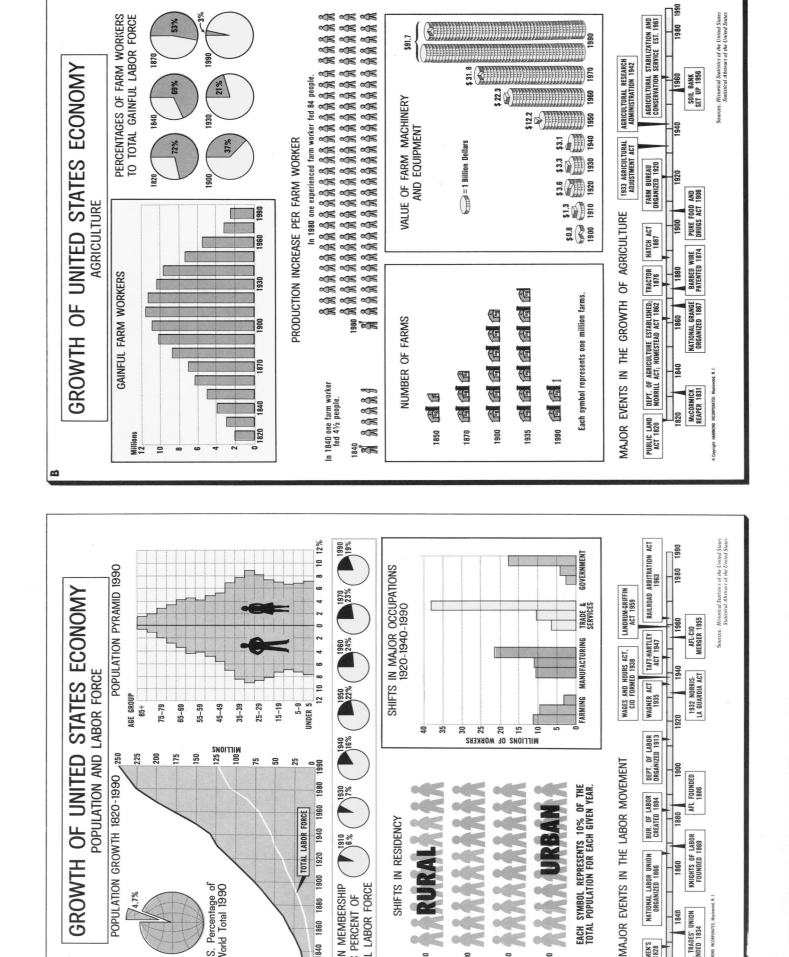

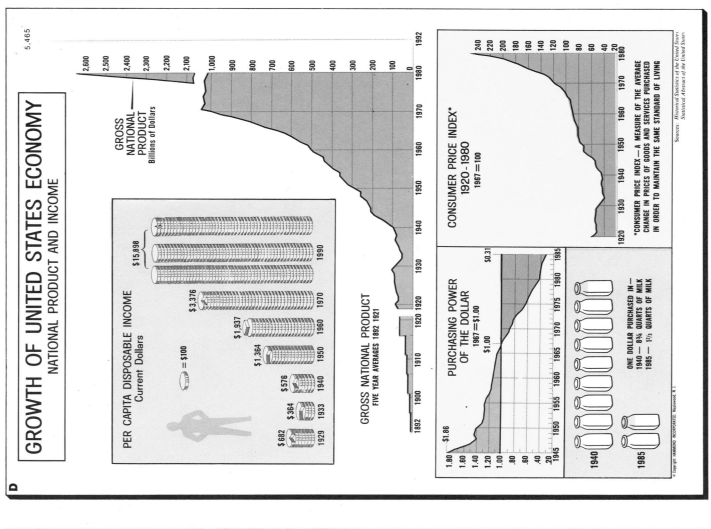

GROWTH OF UNITED STATES ECONOMY
NATIONAL PRODUCT AND INCOME

GROSS NATIONAL PRODUCT
Billions of Dollars

PER CAPITA DISPOSABLE INCOME
Current Dollars

= $100

$15,898   1990
$3,376   1970
$1,937   1960
$1,364   1950
$576   1940
$364   1933
$682   1929

GROSS NATIONAL PRODUCT
FIVE YEAR AVERAGES 1892 1921

CONSUMER PRICE INDEX*
1920-1980
1967 = 100

*CONSUMER PRICE INDEX — A MEASURE OF THE AVERAGE CHANGE IN PRICES OF GOODS AND SERVICES PURCHASED IN ORDER TO MAINTAIN THE SAME STANDARD OF LIVING

PURCHASING POWER OF THE DOLLAR
1967 = $1.00

$1.86 $1.00 $0.31

ONE DOLLAR PURCHASED IN—
1940 = 8⅓ QUARTS OF MILK
1985 = 1⅔ QUARTS OF MILK

1940
1985

Sources: Historical Statistics of the United States
Statistical Abstract of the United States

© Copyright HAMMOND INCORPORATED, Maplewood, N.J.

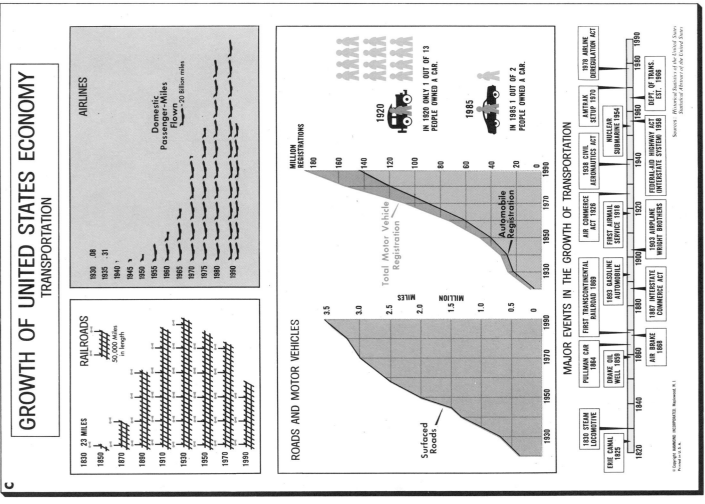

GROWTH OF UNITED STATES ECONOMY
TRANSPORTATION

RAILROADS
50,000 Miles in length

1830 23 MILES
1850
1870
1890
1910
1930
1950
1970
1990

AIRLINES
Domestic Passenger-Miles Flown
= 20 Billion miles

1930 .08
1935 .31
1940
1945
1950
1955
1960
1965
1970
1975
1980
1990

ROADS AND MOTOR VEHICLES

MILLION REGISTRATIONS

Total Motor Vehicle Registration
Automobile Registration

MILES   MILLION
3.5
3.0
2.5
2.0
1.5
1.0
0.5
0

Surfaced Roads

1920
IN 1920 ONLY 1 OUT OF 13 PEOPLE OWNED A CAR.

1985
IN 1985 1 OUT OF 2 PEOPLE OWNED A CAR.

MAJOR EVENTS IN THE GROWTH OF TRANSPORTATION

ERIE CANAL 1825
1830 STEAM LOCOMOTIVE
AIR BRAKE 1868
DRAKE OIL WELL 1859
PULLMAN CAR 1864
FIRST TRANSCONTINENTAL RAILROAD 1869
1887 INTERSTATE COMMERCE ACT
1893 GASOLINE AUTOMOBILE
1903 AIRPLANE WRIGHT BROTHERS
FIRST AIRMAIL SERVICE 1918
AIR COMMERCE ACT 1926
1938 CIVIL AERONAUTICS ACT
NUCLEAR SUBMARINE 1954
AMTRAK SETUP 1970
1978 AIRLINE DEREGULATION ACT
FEDERAL-AID HIGHWAY ACT (INTERSTATE SYSTEM) 1956
DEPT. OF TRANS. EST. 1966

1820 1840 1860 1880 1900 1920 1940 1960 1980 1990

Sources: Historical Statistics of the United States
Statistical Abstract of the United States

© Copyright HAMMOND INCORPORATED, Maplewood, N.J.
Printed in U.S.A.

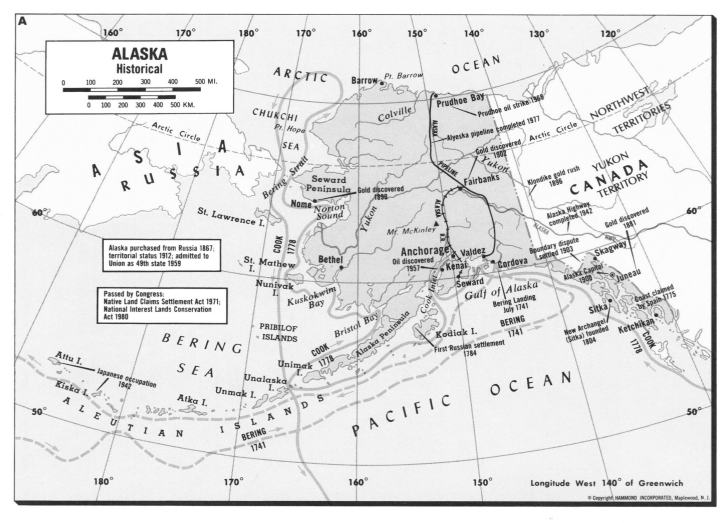

A

ALASKA
Historical

Scale bars:
0 100 200 300 400 500 MI.
0 100 200 300 400 500 KM.

Alaska purchased from Russia 1867; territorial status 1912; admitted to Union as 49th state 1959

Passed by Congress: Native Land Claims Settlement Act 1971; National Interest Lands Conservation Act 1980

ARCTIC OCEAN
Pt. Barrow
Barrow
Prudhoe Bay
Prudhoe oil strike 1968
Colville
Alyeska pipeline completed 1977
NORTHWEST TERRITORIES
CHUKCHI SEA
Pt. Hope
Arctic Circle
Gold discovered 1902
Yukon
Arctic Circle
Bering Strait
Seward Peninsula
Gold discovered 1899
Fairbanks
Klondike gold rush 1896
YUKON TERRITORY
CANADA
Nome
Norton Sound
Alaska Highway completed 1942
St. Lawrence I.
Gold discovered 1881
ASIA
RUSSIA
Mt. McKinley
Boundary dispute settled 1903
Skagway
St. Mathew I.
Bethel
COOK 1778
Anchorage
Oil discovered 1957
Valdez
Kenai
Cordova
Alaska Capital 1900
Juneau
Nunivak I.
Seward
Gulf of Alaska
Coast claimed by Spain 1775
Kuskokwim Bay
Cook Inlet
Bering Landing July 1741
Sitka
New Archangel (Sitka) founded 1804
PRIBILOF ISLANDS
Bristol Bay
Kodiak I.
BERING 1741
Ketchikan
COOK 1778
COOK 1778
Alaska Peninsula
First Russian settlement 1784
BERING SEA
Unimak I.
Attu I.
Japanese occupation 1942
Unalaska I.
Kiska I.
Unmak I.
Atka I.
ALEUTIAN ISLANDS
BERING 1741
PACIFIC OCEAN

Longitude West 140° of Greenwich

© Copyright HAMMOND INCORPORATED, Maplewood, N.J.

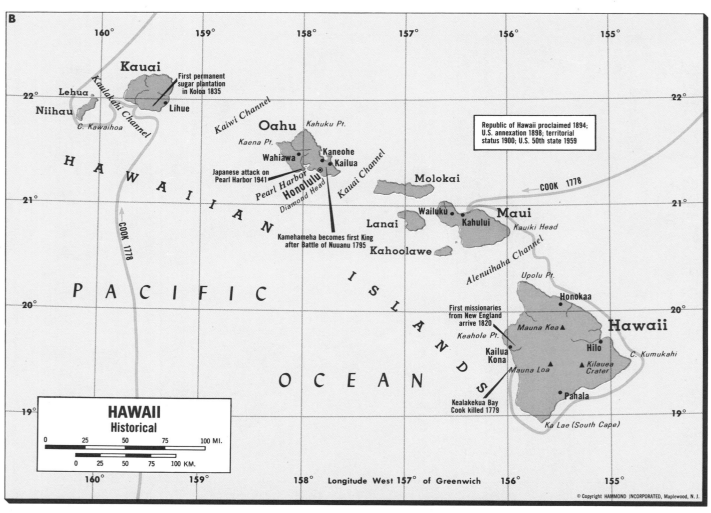

B

Kauai
First permanent sugar plantation in Koloa 1835
Lehua
Lihue
Niihau
Kaulakahi Channel
C. Kawaihoa
Kaiwi Channel
Oahu
Kahuku Pt.
Kaena Pt.
Wahiawa
Kaneohe
Kailua
Japanese attack on Pearl Harbor 1941
Pearl Harbor
Honolulu
Diamond Head
Kauai Channel
Molokai
COOK 1778
Republic of Hawaii proclaimed 1894; U.S. annexation 1898; territorial status 1900; U.S. 50th state 1959
HAWAIIAN
Kamehameha becomes first King after Battle of Nuuanu 1795
Lanai
Wailuku
Kahului
Maui
Kauiki Head
COOK 1778
Kahoolawe
Alenuihaha Channel
Upolu Pt.
ISLANDS
First missionaries from New England arrive 1820
Honokaa
PACIFIC
Mauna Kea
Hawaii
Keahole Pt.
Kailua Kona
Hilo
C. Kumukahi
Mauna Loa
Kilauea Crater
OCEAN
Kealakekua Bay Cook killed 1779
Pahala
Ka Lae (South Cape)

HAWAII
Historical

Scale bars:
0 25 50 75 100 MI.
0 25 50 75 100 KM.

Longitude West 157° of Greenwich

© Copyright HAMMOND INCORPORATED, Maplewood, N.J.

A

THE FIFTY STATES

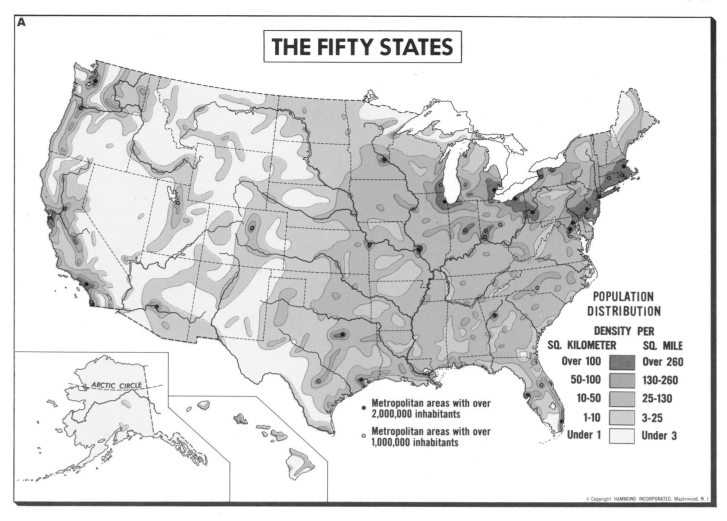

ARCTIC CIRCLE

POPULATION DISTRIBUTION

DENSITY PER

SQ. KILOMETER	SQ. MILE
Over 100	Over 260
50-100	130-260
10-50	25-130
1-10	3-25
Under 1	Under 3

● Metropolitan areas with over 2,000,000 inhabitants

○ Metropolitan areas with over 1,000,000 inhabitants

© Copyright HAMMOND INCORPORATED. Maplewood, N. J.

B

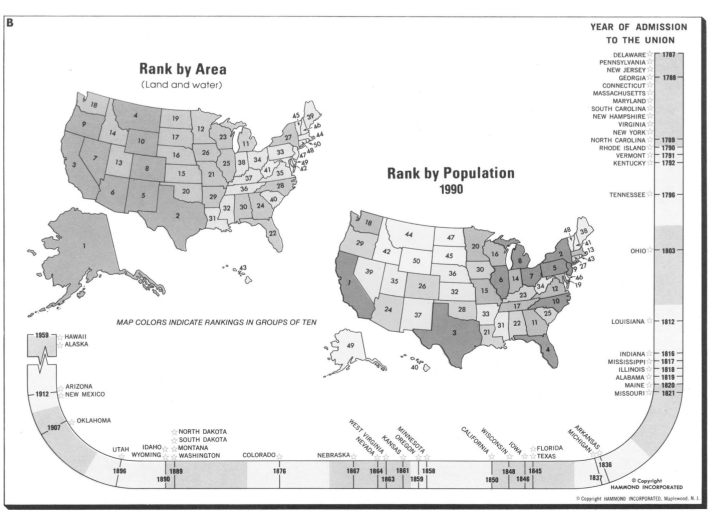

Rank by Area
(Land and water)

Rank by Population
1990

MAP COLORS INDICATE RANKINGS IN GROUPS OF TEN

YEAR OF ADMISSION TO THE UNION

DELAWARE ☆	1787
PENNSYLVANIA ☆	
NEW JERSEY ☆	
GEORGIA ☆	1788
CONNECTICUT ☆	
MASSACHUSETTS ☆	
MARYLAND ☆	
SOUTH CAROLINA ☆	
NEW HAMPSHIRE ☆	
VIRGINIA ☆	
NEW YORK ☆	
NORTH CAROLINA ☆	1789
RHODE ISLAND ☆	1790
VERMONT ☆	1791
KENTUCKY ☆	1792
TENNESSEE ☆	1796
OHIO ☆	1803
LOUISIANA ☆	1812
INDIANA ☆	1816
MISSISSIPPI ☆	1817
ILLINOIS ☆	1818
ALABAMA ☆	1819
MAINE ☆	1820
MISSOURI ☆	1821

1959 ☆ HAWAII
☆ ALASKA

1912 ☆ ARIZONA
☆ NEW MEXICO

☆ OKLAHOMA
1907

☆ NORTH DAKOTA
☆ SOUTH DAKOTA
IDAHO ☆ ☆ MONTANA
UTAH ☆
WYOMING ☆ ☆ WASHINGTON

COLORADO ☆

WEST VIRGINIA ☆
NEVADA ☆
NEBRASKA ☆
KANSAS ☆
OREGON ☆
MINNESOTA ☆

CALIFORNIA ☆
WISCONSIN ☆
IOWA ☆
FLORIDA ☆
TEXAS ☆
ARKANSAS ☆
MICHIGAN ☆

| 1896 | 1889 | 1876 | 1867 | 1864 | 1861 | 1858 | 1848 | 1845 | 1836 |
| 1890 | | | | 1863 | 1859 | | 1850 | 1846 | 1837 |

© Copyright HAMMOND INCORPORATED

© Copyright HAMMOND INCORPORATED, Maplewood, N. J.

POPULATION CHARACTERISTICS

BIRTH AND DEATH RATES
(RATE PER 1,000 POPULATION)

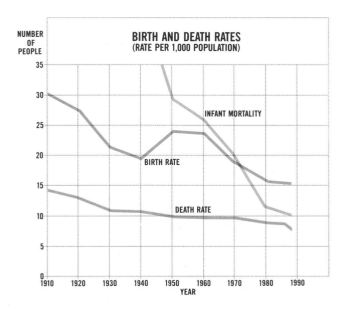

LIFE EXPECTANCY
(MALE AND FEMALE)

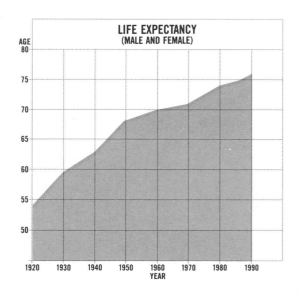

POPULATION SHIFT
1970–1980

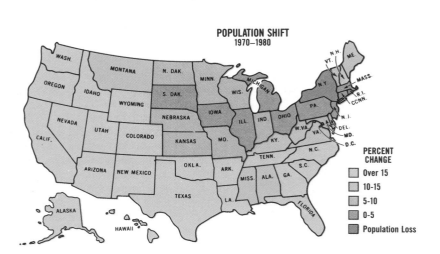

PERCENT CHANGE
- Over 15
- 10-15
- 5-10
- 0-5
- Population Loss

POPULATION PER SQUARE MILE OF LAND AREA
(1790–1990)

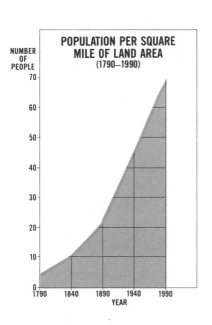

POPULATION SHIFT
1980–1990

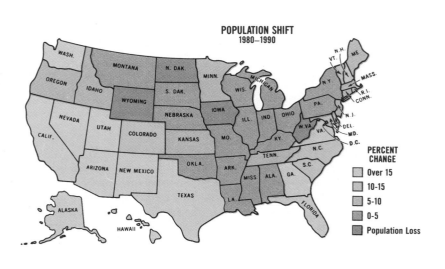

PERCENT CHANGE
- Over 15
- 10-15
- 5-10
- 0-5
- Population Loss

TOTAL POPULATION
(1790–1990)

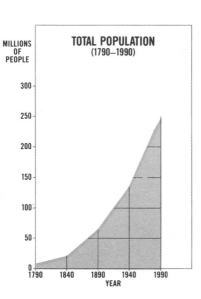

Source: *Statistical Abstract of the United States*

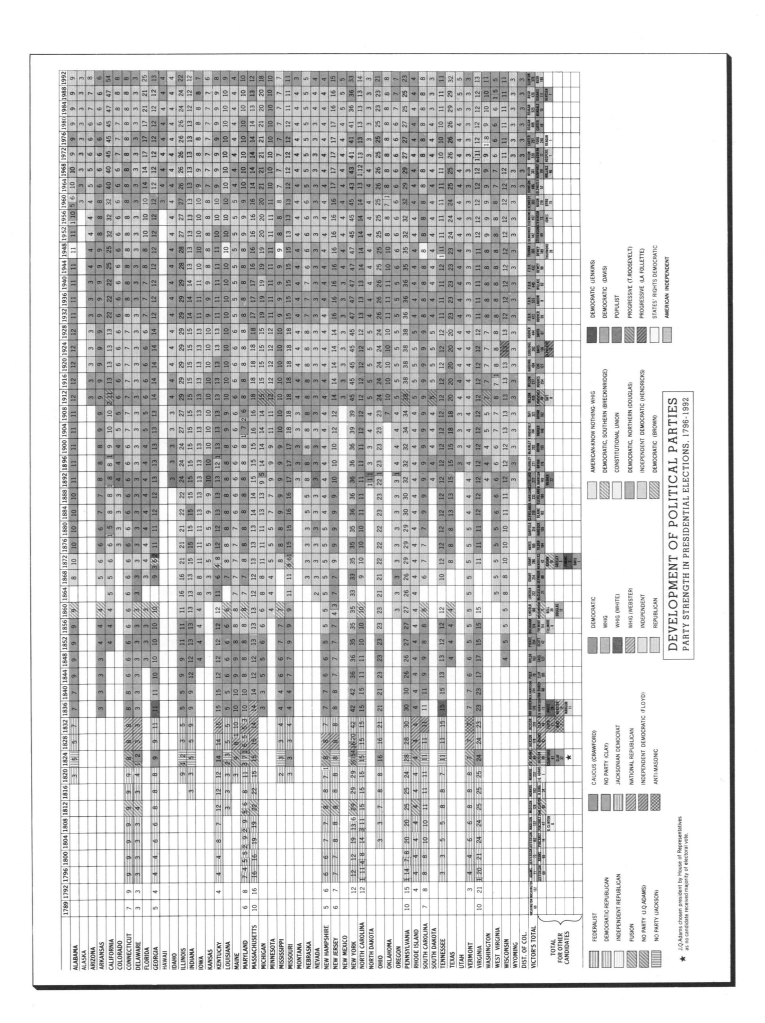

DEVELOPMENT OF POLITICAL PARTIES
PARTY STRENGTH IN PRESIDENTIAL ELECTIONS, 1796–1992

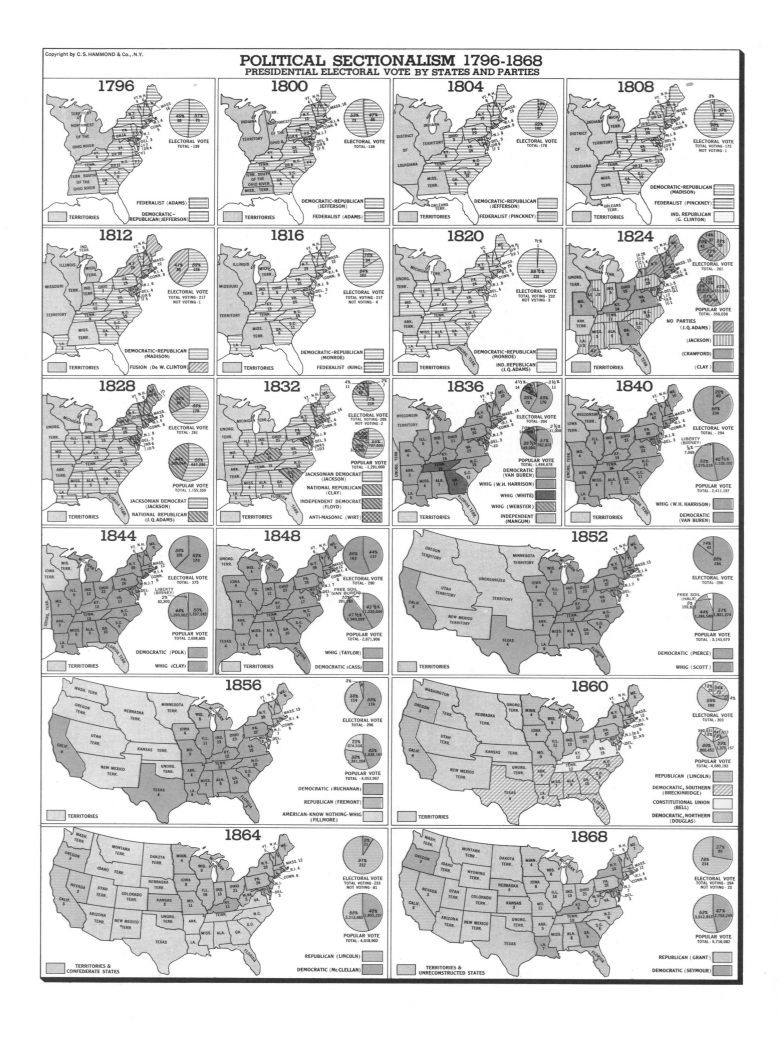

POLITICAL SECTIONALISM 1872-1916
PRESIDENTIAL ELECTORAL VOTE BY STATES AND PARTIES

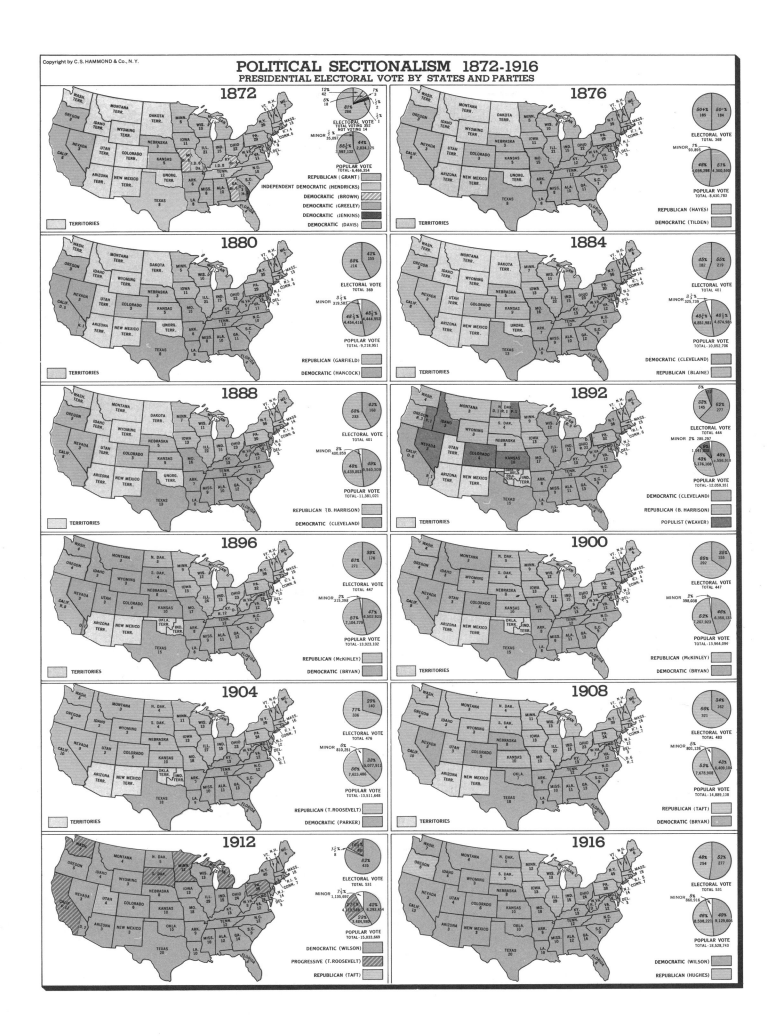

POLITICAL SECTIONALISM 1920-1964
PRESIDENTIAL ELECTORAL VOTE BY STATES AND PARTIES

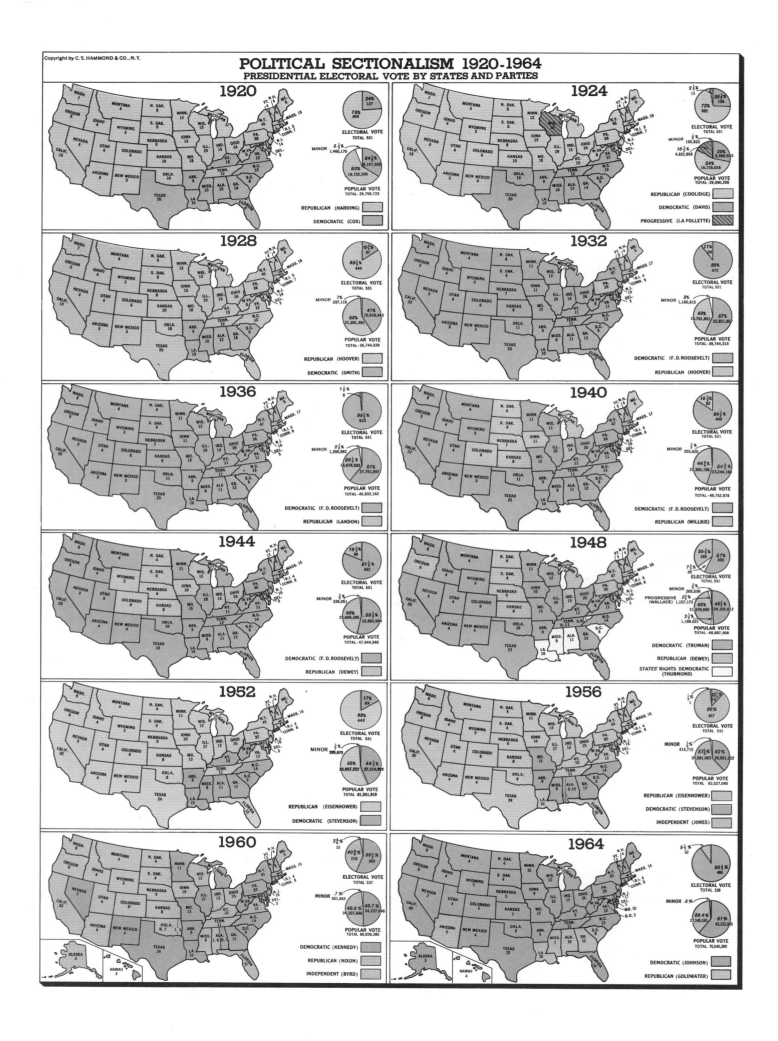

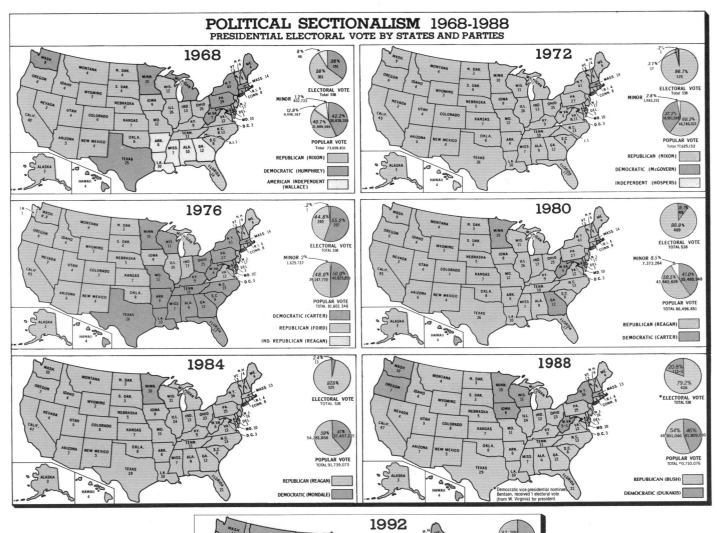

POLITICAL SECTIONALISM 1968-1988
PRESIDENTIAL ELECTORAL VOTE BY STATES AND PARTIES

PRESIDENTS OF THE UNITED STATES

No.	Name	Politics	Native State	Age at Inauguration	Age at Death	No.	Name	Politics	Native State	Age at Inauguration	Age at Death
1	George Washington	Federalist	Va.	57	67	22	Grover Cleveland	Democrat	N.J.	47	71
2	John Adams	Federalist	Mass.	61	90	23	Benjamin Harrison	Republican	Ohio	55	67
3	Thomas Jefferson	Rep.-Dem.	Va.	57	83	24	Grover Cleveland	Democrat	N.J.	55	71
4	James Madison	Rep.-Dem.	Va.	57	85	25	William McKinley	Republican	Ohio	54	58
5	James Monroe	Rep.-Dem.	Va.	58	73	26	Theodore Roosevelt	Republican	N.Y.	42	60
6	John Quincy Adams	Rep.-Dem.	Mass.	57	80	27	William Howard Taft	Republican	Ohio	51	72
7	Andrew Jackson	Democrat	S.C.	61	78	28	Woodrow Wilson	Democrat	Va.	56	67
8	Martin Van Buren	Democrat	N.Y.	54	79	29	Warren G. Harding	Republican	Ohio	55	57
9	William Henry Harrison	Whig	Va.	68	68	30	Calvin Coolidge	Republican	Vt.	51	60
10	John Tyler	Whig	Va.	51	71	31	Herbert Clark Hoover	Republican	Iowa	54	90
11	James Knox Polk	Democrat	N.C.	49	53	32	Franklin D. Roosevelt	Democrat	N.Y.	51	63
12	Zachary Taylor	Whig	Va.	64	65	33	Harry S Truman	Democrat	Mo.	60	88
13	Millard Fillmore	Whig	N.Y.	50	74	34	Dwight D. Eisenhower	Republican	Texas	62	78
14	Franklin Pierce	Democrat	N.H.	48	64	35	John F. Kennedy	Democrat	Mass.	43	46
15	James Buchanan	Democrat	Pa.	65	77	36	Lyndon B. Johnson	Democrat	Texas	55	64
16	Abraham Lincoln	Republican	Ky.	52	56	37	Richard M. Nixon	Republican	Calif.	56	—
17	Andrew Johnson	Democrat	N.C.	56	66	38	Gerald R. Ford	Republican	Mich.	61	—
18	Ulysses Simpson Grant	Republican	Ohio	46	63	39	James E. Carter, Jr.	Democrat	Ga.	52	—
19	Rutherford B. Hayes	Republican	Ohio	54	70	40	Ronald W. Reagan	Republican	Ill.	69	—
20	James Abram Garfield	Republican	Ohio	49	49	41	George H. W. Bush	Republican	Mass.	64	—
21	Chester Alan Arthur	Republican	Vt.	50	56	42	William J. Clinton	Democrat	Ark.	46	—

Flags of American History

FLAGS OF DISCOVERY AND SETTLEMENT

FLAG OF LEIF ERICKSON—1000
RAVEN OF THE VIKINGS, FIRST FLAG CARRIED
TO AMERICA'S SHORES.

**EXPEDITIONARY FLAG OF COLUMBUS
1492**

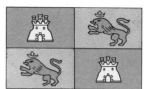

FLAG OF COLUMBUS 1492—1498
STANDARD OF FERDINAND AND ISABELLA.
RAISED AT SAN SALVADOR 1492, MAINLAND, 1498.

FLAG OF JOHN CABOT—1497
CROSS OF ST. GEORGE. FIRST FLAG RAISED
ON MAINLAND. RALEIGH'S FLAG 1585.

FLAG OF CHAMPLAIN—1603
BORNE BY CARTIER, JOLIET, MARQUETTE, LA SALLE
AND OTHER INTREPID FRENCH VOYAGEURS.

FLAG OF HUDSON—1607
FIRST FLAG RAISED AT NEW YORK, VERRAZANO DIS-
COVERED THE RIVER EIGHTY FOUR YEARS EARLIER.

FLAG OF THE MAYFLOWER—1620
FLAG BORNE ON THE MAIN MAST OF THE MAYFLOWER
BY THE PILGRIM FATHERS.

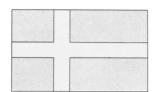

FLAG OF SWEDEN—1638
ENSIGN OF NEW SWEDEN RAISED ON THE
DELAWARE RIVER.

FLAGS OF COLONIAL DAYS

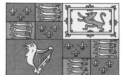

STUART STANDARD 1603—1649, 1660—1689

CROMWELL'S STANDARD 1653—1660

ROYAL STANDARD 1689—1702

ROYAL STANDARD 1707—1714

ROYAL STANDARD 1714—1801

ENGLISH RED ENSIGN
THE FAMOUS METEOR FLAG OF OLD ENGLAND
AND ENSIGN OF COLONIES 17th CENTURY.

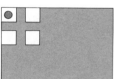

ENDICOTT FLAG—1634
THE SALEM ENSIGN SHOWING RELIGIOUS
OPPOSITION TO CROSS IN CANTON.

THREE COUNTY TROUP—1659
FLAG OF THE THREE MASSACHUSETTS COUNTIES
AND EMBLEM OF KING PHILIP'S WAR, 1675—1676.

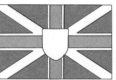

ESCUTCHEONED JACK—1701
FLAG DESIGNED FOR MERCHANT SHIPS
OF HIS MAJESTY'S PLANTATIONS.

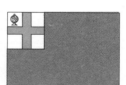

NEW ENGLAND FLAG—1737
THIS ENSIGN SHOWS THE EARLY TENDENCY
OF THE COLONIES TO FIND INDIVIDUAL FLAGS.

FLAGS OF THE REVOLUTION

TAUNTON FLAG—1774
JNE OF THE EARLIEST EMBLEMS
OF THE REVOLUTION.

BEDFORD FLAG—1775
CARRIED BY REVERE AND DAWES
IN AROUSING THE MINUTE MEN.

CULPEPER FLAG—1775
ONE OF THE EARLY RATTLESNAKE FLAGS
CARRIED BY THE MINUTE MEN.

PHILADELPHIA LIGHT HORSE
WASHINGTON'S ESCORT TO COMMAND
OF THE CONTINENTAL ARMY, 1775.

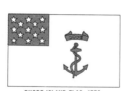

RHODE ISLAND FLAG—1776
CARRIED AT BRANDYWINE, TRENTON AND
YORKTOWN.

FORT MOULTRIE FLAG—1776
NAILED TO STAFF BY SERGEANT JASPER
WHEN SHOT AWAY.

LIBERTY TREE FLAG—1776
THE PINE TREE COMES FROM COINS OF THE
COLONY OF MASSACHUSETTS, 1652.

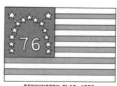

BENNINGTON FLAG—1777
FLAG OF VICTORY OF THE GREEN MOUNTAIN
BOYS.

BENJAMIN FRANKLIN FLAG
ALSO CALLED "SERAPIS" FLAG. GENERALLY ACCEPTED AS
ORIGINATED BY BENJAMIN FRANKLIN AT COURT OF LOUIS XVI.

MERCHANT ENSIGN 1776—1795
AN EMBLEM IN GENERAL USE, ALSO
PRIVATEER'S FLAG.

FLAGS OF THE OLD NAVY

GADSDEN FLAG—1775
COMMODORE ESEK HOPKINS' ENSIGN USED IN HIS FIRST
FLEET COMMAND.

WASHINGTON'S NAVY ENSIGN—1775
THE FLAG OF THE SIX CRUISERS THAT FORMED THE FIRST
AMERICAN NAVAL FLEET.

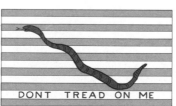

FIRST NAVY JACK—1775
HOSTED AT THE MAIN MAST BY COMMANDER-IN-CHIEF ESEK HOPKINS,
DECEMBER 3, 1775.

FLAGS OF THE YOUNG REPUBLIC

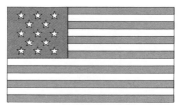

FIRST NAVY STARS AND STRIPES
IN ABSENCE OF SPECIFIC ARRANGEMENT OF STARS BY CONGRESS JUNE 14, 1777 IT WAS CUSTOMARY FOR NAVY TO PLACE THE STARS IN FORM OF CROSSES OF ST. GEORGE AND ST. ANDREW.

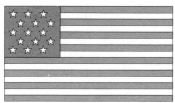

"STAR SPANGLED BANNER"—1814
THE EMBLEM OF INSPIRATION OF OUR NATIONAL ANTHEM, 1814. FLAG OF VICTORY OVER BARBARY PIRATES 1803 TO 1805.

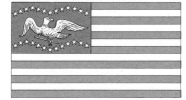

FREMONT THE PATHFINDER'S FLAG—40'S
EMBLEM THAT BLAZED THE TRAIL FOR THE COVERED WAGON IN THE ROARING 40'S. THE EARLY ENSIGN OF THE PLAINS.

FAMOUS BATTLE FLAGS

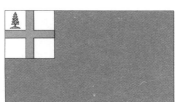

BUNKER HILL FLAG—1775
HISTORIC EMBLEM THAT PROVED THE STRENGTH OF THE SPIRIT OF AMERICAN LIBERTY. CARRIED AT LEXINGTON AND CONCORD.

CAMBRIDGE FLAG, FIRST NAVY ENSIGN 1775—1776
HOISTED BY JOHN PAUL JONES, DECEMBER 3, 1775 AND BY GENERAL WASHINGTON, JANUARY 2, 1776.

CONTINENTAL FLAG
CARRIED IN 1775–1777, SHOWING PINE TREE, SYMBOL OF MASSACHUSETTS BAY COLONY, IN PLACE OF THE CROSSES OF ST. GEORGE AND ST. ANDREW.

FLAGS OF THE CONFEDERACY

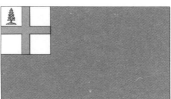

FIRST CONFEDERATE FLAG
FAMOUS "STARS AND BARS" USED FROM MARCH 1861 TO MAY 1863.

SECOND CONFEDERATE FLAG
NATIONAL EMBLEM FROM MAY 1, 1863 TO MARCH 4, 1865.

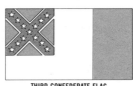

THIRD CONFEDERATE FLAG
NATIONAL EMBLEM ADOPTED MARCH 8, 1865.

CONFEDERATE NAVY FLAG
USED FROM MAY 1, 1863 TO END OF WAR, 1865. THE BATTLE FLAG WAS SQUARE.

OTHER NOTEWORTHY FLAGS OF AMERICAN HISTORY

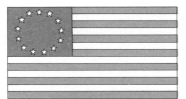

FIRST STARS AND STRIPES
UNITED EMBLEM OF INDEPENDENCE SAID TO HAVE ORIGINATED BY GEORGE WASHINGTON FOLLOWING ACT OF CONGRESS OF JUNE 14, 1777.

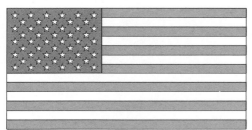

PRESENT DAY FLAG

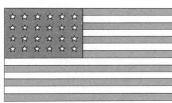

"OLD GLORY"
NAME GIVEN BY CAPTAIN WILLIAM DRIVER, COMMANDING THE BRIG "CHARLES DAGGETT" IN 1831.

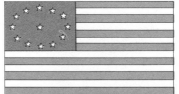

FLAG OF THE THIRD MARYLAND REGIMENT—1778
CARRIED AT THE BATTLE OF COWPENS JANUARY, 1778 AND USED AS COLORS OF AMERICAN LAND FORCES UNTIL MEXICAN WAR.

NAPOLEON'S LOUISIANA FLAG
THIS FLAG WAS REPLACED BY "STARS AND STRIPES" FOLLOWING LOUISIANA PURCHASE DECEMBER 24, 1803.

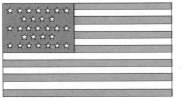

U.S. NAVY JACK
USED BY NAVAL VESSELS AND MARITIME GOVERNORS.

FLAG OF THE WAR OF 1812 (1812—1814)
SHOWING FIFTEEN STARS AND FIFTEEN BARS AS CHANGED UPON ADMISSION OF VERMONT.

RUSSIAN AMERICAN CO'S. FLAG
EMBLEM RAISED 1799, REPLACED BY "STARS AND STRIPES" 1867.

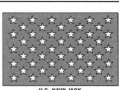

U.S. COAST GUARD FLAG
WITHOUT EMBLEM ON FLY THIS IS U.S. CUSTOMS FLAG.

FLAG OF THE MEXICAN WAR—1845
NOT ACTUALLY USED AS REGIMENTAL COLORS BY TROOPS, BUT AS FLAG OF CONQUEST AND OCCUPATION.

FLAG OF THE CIVIL WAR 1861—1865
THE "STARS AND STRIPES" WITH THIRTY SIX STARS IN THE UNION CARRIED BY THE NORTHERN ARMIES DURING LATER YEARS OF THE CIVIL WAR.

THE FLAG OF 1818
SHOWING RETURN TO THIRTEEN STRIPES AND ADDITIONAL STARS IN CANTON.

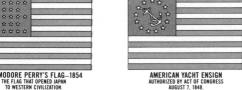

COMMODORE PERRY'S FLAG—1854
THE FLAG THAT OPENED JAPAN TO WESTERN CIVILIZATION.

AMERICAN YACHT ENSIGN
AUTHORIZED BY ACT OF CONGRESS AUGUST 7, 1848.

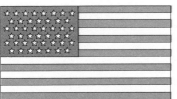

FLAG OF THE SPANISH-AMERICAN WAR—1898
THE EMBLEM OF LIBERTY THAT BROUGHT FREEDOM TO CUBA.

BRITISH COLUMBIA
ALBERTA
SASKATCHEWAN
MANITOBA
WASHINGTON
OREGON
IDAHO
MONTANA
WYOMING
NORTH DAKOTA
SOUTH DAKOTA
NEBRASKA
CALIFORNIA
NEVADA
UTAH
COLORADO
KANSAS
ARIZONA
NEW MEXICO
OKLAHOMA
TEXAS
MEXICO
BAJA CALIFORNIA
CHIHUAHUA
COAHUILA
PACIFIC OCEAN
GULF OF CALIFORNIA
ROCKY MTS.
Vancouver
Seattle
Portland
Spokane
Boise
Salt Lake City
Denver
San Francisco
Sacramento
Fresno
LOS ANGELES
San Diego
Las Vegas
Phoenix
Tucson
Albuquerque
Santa Fe
El Paso
Calgary
Edmonton
Regina
Cheyenne
Helena
MISSOURI
ILLINOIS
St. Louis
Cincinnati
SCALE OF MILES
ALASKA
RUSSIA
YUKON TERRITORY
BRITISH COLUMBIA
BERING SEA
ARCTIC OCEAN
Anchorage
Fairbanks
Juneau
Nome
Aleutian Is.
HAWAII
Honolulu
Oahu
Kauai
Molokai
Maui
Hawaii
Tropic of Cancer
Longitude West of Greenwich
Berkeley
Oakland
San Jose
Long Beach
Pasadena
Santa Monica

UNITED STATES

POLYCONIC PROJECTION
SCALE OF MILES
0   50   100   200   300
SCALE OF KILOMETRES
0   50 100   200   300

Capitals of Countries _ _ _ _ _ _ _ _ _ ☆
State and Provincial Capitals _ _ _ _ _ _ △
International Boundaries _ _ _ _ _ _ _ _ _
State and Provincial Boundaries _ _ _ _ _

Copyright by C. S. HAMMOND & CO., N.Y.

Longitude West of Greenwich

Flags of States, Territories and Possessions

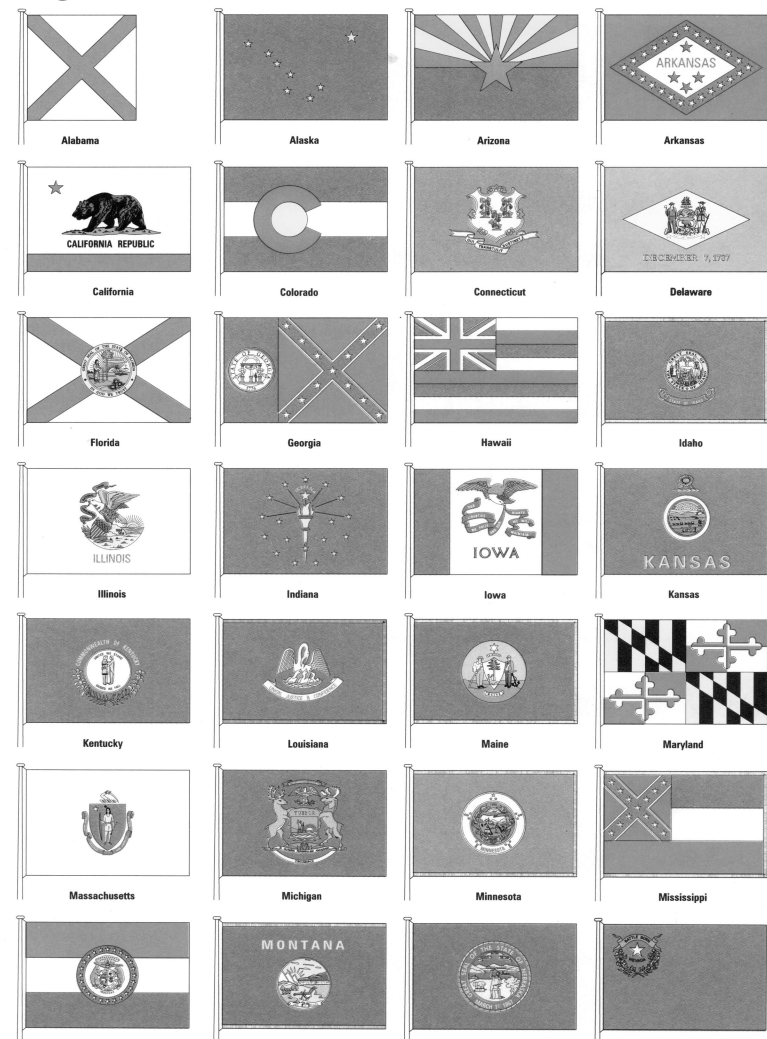

Alabama	Alaska	Arizona	Arkansas
California	Colorado	Connecticut	Delaware
Florida	Georgia	Hawaii	Idaho
Illinois	Indiana	Iowa	Kansas
Kentucky	Louisiana	Maine	Maryland
Massachusetts	Michigan	Minnesota	Mississippi
Missouri	Montana	Nebraska	Nevada

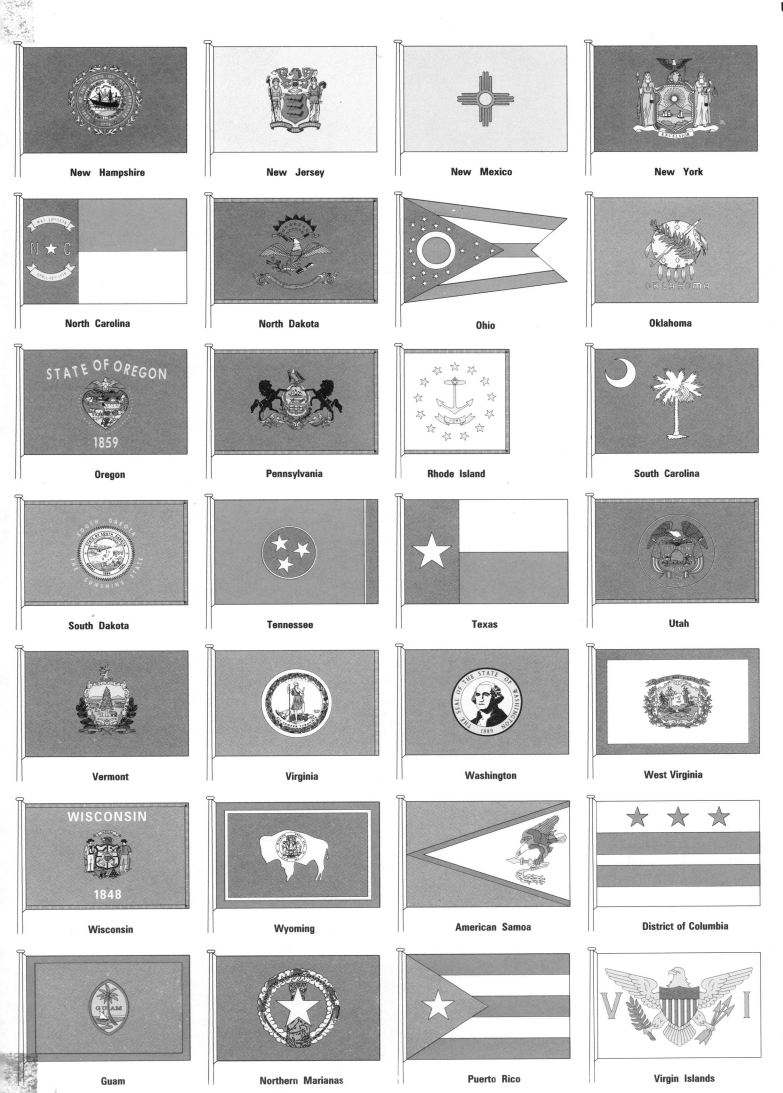

New Hampshire	New Jersey	New Mexico	New York
North Carolina	North Dakota	Ohio	Oklahoma
Oregon	Pennsylvania	Rhode Island	South Carolina
South Dakota	Tennessee	Texas	Utah
Vermont	Virginia	Washington	West Virginia
Wisconsin	Wyoming	American Samoa	District of Columbia
Guam	Northern Marianas	Puerto Rico	Virgin Islands

Index

This index lists historically important places, areas, events and geographical features appearing on the maps of the United States History Atlas. Each entry is followed by the page number on which the name appears. The letters following the page number designate a particular map on pages containing more than one map. Names that appear on more than one map are indexed to the map or maps portraying the place at its most historically significant period.